PARENTAL STRESS
C E N T R E

A PARENT'S GUIDE TO FINDING YOUR LOST IDENTITY

AND DISCOVERING YOUR PERSONAL PEACE

JACKIE HALL

Disclaimer: The intent of this author is only to offer information of a general nature to help you in your quest for emotional well-being. It is not intended to be a substitute for any psychological, financial, legal, or any other professional advice. In the event you use any of the information in this book for yourself, the author and publisher assume no responsibility for your actions. If expert assistance or counselling is needed, the services of a competent medical or psychological professional should be sought.

First published 2013

Designed and typeset by Vicki Gauci

Cover design by Roland Ali Pantin
Edited by Louise Johnson

ISBN 978 0 9875433 2 5

Table of Contents

Introduction.. 1

Chapter One – Who am I? 7

Chapter Two – The Mind TRACK to Happiness Process 29

Chapter Three – Step One of the Mind TRACK to
Happiness Process.. 34

    Exercise One
    What identity am I attached to and where did I learn to
    attach it to my self-worth?.. 42

    Exercise Two
    Naming my identity... 56

Chapter Four – Step Two of the Mind TRACK
to Happiness Process 57

    Exercise Three
    Evidence of your life having highs AND lows......................... 64

    Exercise Four
    Find the hidden good in the bad... 72

    Exercise Five
    Evidence of your worth.. 95

    Exercise Six
    Create a new story 104

Chapter Five – Step Three: Aim – What do I want?............. 106

    Exercise Seven
    Write your eulogy.. 116

Chapter Six – Step Four: Choices – How do I get what I want?... 118

Exercise Eight
Make time for research.. 122

Chapter Seven – Step Five: Know your plan and action it... 124

Exercise Nine
What is your plan?... 125

Chapter Eight – Just be YOU 128

Introduction

"I don't know who I am anymore?"

This is often the catch cry of new parents. Consumed by the huge impact the changes having children bring to our lives, we can feel lost between the world we used to know and this strange new world. Often life feels like an endless stream of work, with little sleep and no fun.

In the early stages of having children, or even years after, parents can feel a bit lost – not knowing who they are, what they want out of life – or they may even begin to question what life is all about.

Your old ways of doing things don't fit into life with children and you may find you have no desire to live life that old way anymore. The problem is you're not sure what other way there is to live.

I have experienced firsthand what it's like to feel as if you've lost yourself to the role of being a parent. At one point being a mum had totally consumed me and 'my life' seemed to have slipped away leaving depression in its place.

I felt like a slave. It was like one day just rolled into the next and all of them were the same. Nappies, crying, sleep routines, mess, cleaning and cooking and very little time for me. Hubby became the help that walked through the door of an evening rather than the love of my life. On and on it went, never feeling like there was an end to the workload and having minimal fun in the process.

It left me asking myself: "surely this isn't all there is to life as a parent?"

Mums aren't the only ones to feel this way though. For Dads, the feeling can also be quite similar.

The parent who works outside the home can feel like a slave to their work as well. The pressure to make ends meet on one income, coming home to the worst hours of the day when the kids are tired and hungry, dealing with an equally tired and snappy partner, surviving on next to no sleep, struggling with pent up anger and frustration from exhaustion and impatience, and generally feeling like the 'old me' who used to have interests and hobbies has disappeared.

Dads can wind up feeling like they're just unappreciated money-making working machines.

Feeling this way about parenthood can lead either mum or dad into depression if you can't find a way out of it.

Thankfully, there is a way out and that's what this book is going to teach you.

The reality of parenting is that it's full on sometimes. There are many sacrifices and changes that need to be made, both literally and mentally.

However, when it comes to how you feel about your life, the only reason why you feel you have lost your identity is because you've lost sight of what your identity is now you are a parent.

You're stuck on your old reference point of 'who I am' and this may be in conflict with the reality that your old ideas about 'me' are simply not compatible with your current circumstances. Parenting literally changes the core of who you are in so many ways. It is imperative you take some time to deliberately reassess yourself and embark on a little self-discovery.

Think about it for a moment. Since having your first baby absolutely everything in your life has changed or at the very least been altered to fit around your new lifestyle – your physical body changes (for women), the way you see the world changes, who you interact with can change and how you socialise. Your priorities have changed and what drives your decisions. What you wear, what you talk about and how you behave often changes too.

Sometimes past issues buried deep within you may begin to rear their ugly heads. You may discover some great but also some very nasty characteristics to your personality you never knew existed.

Sometimes the bigger questions start to become more important, like why am I here? What is my purpose? What do I believe in when it comes to the bigger picture, and what am I going to teach my children as their belief/faith?

3

You might begin to question your capabilities for raising a healthy, happy child. You may worry about your own fears and insecurities and wonder how you are going to teach your child to feel happy about their life when you don't even know how to do that yourself.

You may be determined to be a completely different parent to your own parents yet find that you continually wind up doing the exact things you said you'd never do.

When you become a parent you need to reconsider how you now fit into the world, especially if your old identity was attached to your career or an interest you are no longer able to pursue, or at least not with the spontaneity you used to.

In short, becoming a parent will have changed you physically, mentally, emotionally, spiritually, morally and ethically to some degree. This is a huge transition in your life, and not one that can be idly surpassed without some deliberate reflection and personal re-alignment.

Becoming a parent, although exhausting at first and confusing for you personally, is an opportunity to give your perspective on life a complete makeover.

Society as a whole is at a turning point. There is a rising trend of stress, depression and anxiety, but people are starting to realise it doesn't have to be this way. They are starting to seek help on how to think and feel differently and changes are starting to happen in society.

As parents we are a massive influencer of this much needed mind shift in society because we are raising the future generation.

To help your children to grow into happy, healthy minded human beings, we must learn to become one too. So if you are feeling like you've lost your identity, that's fantastic!

This book is not going to help you to find your identity again. It's going to help you to completely redesign it.

Chapter One

Who Am I?

Consider the statement *'I don't know who I am anymore?'*.

Who is the 'I' that doesn't know and who is the 'I' you don't know anymore? Are they two separate people? When you refer to the word 'I' or 'me', what part of yourself are you actually referring to?

When you say you've lost yourself, what part of yourself do you think you've lost?

And why do you need to know who the 'I' is? What purpose does it serve you to know who 'I' is? How does that benefit your life or make things better?

These are very deep questions and some of them are ones that spiritual, religious and philosophical circles have been trying to answer for centuries.

We now know a lot about how the brain works and we can use this understanding to get a clear picture of why we are so attached to these 'I' and 'me' descriptions of ourselves. This helps us get clear on what part we think we're missing and how we can get this 'me' back (or redefine it, which is what you really need to do).

7

How the brain thinks.

In order to understand why you feel you have lost your identity it's important to understand what your identity was in the first place. To do that we need to understand a little bit about the human brain.

As boring as this might sound I promise to keep it simple and show you the relevance of why you need to know this.

When you are born into this world you have very few neural connections in the brain. Neural connections are organised patterns of electrical pulses that connect one neuron to the next and allow the brain to function the way it does.

Newborns have enough neural connections in the brain to eat, sleep, pump their heart and perform other very basic human functions to stay alive. All other neural connections grow as a result of learning from your environment and the experiences you've had.

This occurs primarily during the ages of zero to seven. By observing the world around you, experiencing it and receiving information from other people you begin to adopt a view of life. You form your opinions and you begin to perceive the world in habitual ways.

The three ways in which you learn to think about the world are;

- through observation,
- self-experience, and
- being convinced by others (who I trust).

Remember these three ways, because I will be referring to them throughout this book. The repetition of receiving the same information in these ways physically creates neural connections in the brain (one thought links to being relevant with the other) and eventually creating neural pathways – a habitual train of thought.

Most of us learn to interpret the world from how you experience your parents. You watch them and their reactions, you experience the cause and effect of their actions and their actions on you, and you listen to what they say. You trust them and see them as experts in the area of life and adopt their views on life.

As you continue to experience the world with the five senses, your brain is continually looking for **evidence** to support the new ideas you are being exposed to. The evidence you find strengthens the neural connections until they become a habitual belief – how you perceive your life. Remember the word evidence too, as I will also be referring to this important concept throughout the book as well.

A perfect example of an idea being first adopted and then reinforced with evidence is the childhood belief in Santa Claus.

What is it that made you take on the idea of Santa Claus to the point of it becoming a belief? What evidence did you have?

You observed the Christmas tree, movies, Santa at the shopping centre, you were convinced by others – your parents, friends other family members, the media etc – and you experienced finding presents under the tree on Christmas day.

All of this evidence supported the belief that Santa Claus is real and you created a neural connection in the brain that linked all of this information into the category Christmas. Even now you can probably conger up a feeling or a memory when you see those little baubles from the tree, or you see the family angel you put on the tree every year.

The brain has learnt to associate Christmas with all those memories and all of the evidence that Santa Claus was real.

During this very tender, naïve age, you essentially created a belief system which contained all your thoughts, views and opinions about life that you use to interpret events and decide on actions.

It's likely you are still operating out of those same beliefs even now you are an adult.

As well as adopting specific views on life, children are also learning how to be in the world. Human beings have a natural instinct to survive and the brain uses your belief system to assess whether something is pleasurable or painful and then decides if it needs to issue a command to the body to do something about it.

This isn't just about survival in terms of life or death, it can also be about emotional survival – the need we all have to be nurtured and protected from emotional harm.

Take a look at this diagram of how all human beings process information.

All humans follow this process

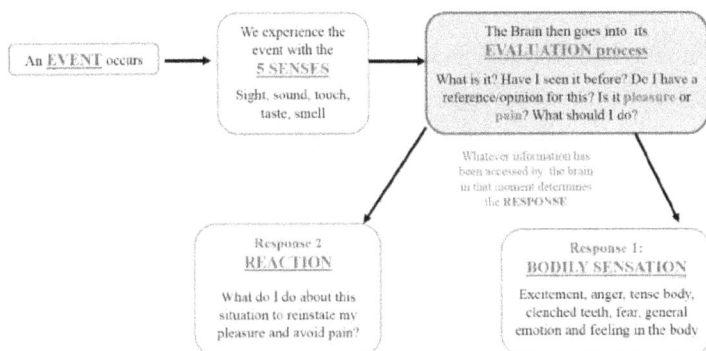

An EVENT occurs	We experience the event with the **5 SENSES** — Sight, sound, touch, taste, smell

The Brain then goes into its **EVALUATION process** — What is it? Have I seen it before? Do I have a reference/opinion for this? Is it pleasure or pain? What should I do?

Whatever information has been accessed by the brain in that moment determines the RESPONSE

Response 2 **REACTION** — What do I do about this situation to reinstate my pleasure and avoid pain?

Response 1: **BODILY SENSATION** — Excitement, anger, tense body, clenched teeth, fear, general emotion and feeling in the body

The behaviour is just the end result. If we want to change the behaviour we have to change the evaluation process!!

You can see here that as a result of the information you receive from the senses, your brain goes into evaluation mode. It asks: What is this I'm seeing, hearing, touching, tasting or smelling (the five senses)? Do I have a reference point for this? Have I seen it before? Where can I link it to?

Your brain has learnt to link bits of information with other bits of information to create neural pathways in the brain.

These pathways are triggered whenever anything relevant gets experienced through the senses.

To get a visual of what is physically happening in your brain, find this You Tube clip – Neural Pathways – Building Self-confidence by Streetwisdom Billy.*

The video only goes for four minutes, but explains very simply how the brain develops. It's valuable for you to visually see what's going on in your brain – and your child's.

Throughout your childhood and beyond the brain is using the senses (sight, sound, touch, taste, smell) to get information about life, then sort it, categorise it, link it and memorise how to respond to it.

You use what you've learnt about life to interpret current events.

Another simple example of this is the memory of a Cocker Spaniel I have from when I was a kid. I have lots of fond memories of this time of my life, but I also have some not so fond memories – like when I watched her get hit by a car. She survived and came back from the vet with three legs, and we went about our lives.

However my memory of the accident, along with the many other experiences I had with her, went into the category of dogs and more specifically Cocker Spaniels. Whenever I see or hear of Cocker Spaniels my brain instantly recalls

* http://www.youtube.com/watch?v=BtP-V_
PYpsg&list=FLLlcjlP8GEMIAfNoX7QpuZQ&index=2

the information of my three legged dog who had the car accident and even recalls the night of the accident, how I felt, what I was thinking and loads of other experiences I had with that dog.

It's an instant response because the brain habitually links all this information as being relevant whenever I see Cocker Spaniels.

This is what we are doing all of the time – thinking in accordance with past information, beliefs, memories and opinions about those memories.

As a result of this thinking, a response is then issued in the body. If I spent long enough recalling that memory and associated thoughts about the night of my dog being hit by a car, I could probably even conger up the same fear and sadness I experienced that night. This is because the brain cannot distinguish between what is real and what is vividly imagined.

So as the process goes, we access our beliefs or thoughts about what we are sensing and produce a physical sensation in the body – emotions. These may be physical sensations in the body like shaking, sweating or increased heart rate. Next the brain tries to distinguish the second response – my reaction: What do I do about this situation?

This is where the brain's instinct to survive kicks in – emotionally and literally.

The main question is: How do I seek pleasure and avoid pain? How do I restore equilibrium to what I have grown to believe is correct about life? It is a fundamental human instinct to follow this process and we are all doing it all the time, both consciously and subconsciously.

The 'what's in it for me' factor is what drives all of the decisions we make and actions we take and it relies on our beliefs – our evaluation process – to decipher how to go about pursuing pleasure, avoiding pain and restoring the equilibrium.

Furthermore the evaluation process is relying on the information received and categorised leading up to right now, so essentially you are constantly assessing life through your past beliefs.

When you apply this understanding of the human brain to your personal identity you can surmise that you are identifying with yourself in accordance with what the brain has learnt to believe about you. You are trying to get back to this learnt way of being, an identity you believe makes your life 'right' and lets you pursue pleasure, avoid pain and restore equilibrium.

Children learn very quickly how to define their roles in the world so they get attention, love, approval, acknowledgement, become part of the family and validate their worth. It's emotional survival. This emotional survival is what I will refer to as self-worth.

Let's take a moment to summarise.

- We learnt about life from our environment as a child and our brain grew physical neural connections in the brain in accordance to the information we received and categorised.

- These neural pathways are your way of interpreting the world and you use it to establish how you fit in with your environment.

- Using this information you have adopted specific beliefs about what you need to DO and BE in order to be worthy.

- This expectation of who you should be is called your identity. It is made up of your beliefs about self. It contains all of your views, opinions and thoughts about who you are, what your life should be like and what needs to be done in order to pursue pleasure, avoid pain and maintain equilibrium.

- The beliefs that define your identity are what is driving all the decisions you make and the actions you take.

However, there is also one more aspect to this brain function that we need to discuss – the mind-body connection.

If you look back on the diagram of the evaluation process I showed you, you can see that by evaluating your life with

15

your learnt beliefs two responses resulted. One of those responses is the bodily response.

Every time you have a thought you release a chemical into the body. What we consciously feel is a chemical response we have come to recognise as 'how I feel', which is a direct result of how you evaluated life in that moment.

Experts say we have 60,000 thoughts a day and 90 percent of them are the same thoughts as yesterday. If you are continuously thinking about how bad your life is, how you are missing out on the life you're supposed to be having, or entering into continuous put downs, over time it becomes a habit to think about yourself this way.

Remember, when your brain has enough evidence from observation, self-experience and being convinced by others, a neural pathway in the brain is formed. Thinking this way results in you feeling the result of this way of thinking day-in and day-out. Your body gets used to those chemicals being released in the body.

Sometimes you aren't even aware of anything in particular that is triggering these feelings. You just feel lost, down, grumpy and low all the time and you just can't seem to shake it off.

Let me explain why this is happening.

You have learnt to adopt beliefs about how life should be. These beliefs have become strong neural pathways in the brain. In effect they are habits of thinking.

For example, you may have come to believe achievements make you valuable. They make you feel like you are important to the world (i.e. they make me feel like I fit in, they make me feel worthy or valuable).

This may have been set up as a child because your parents rewarded you or gave you loads of attention when you were achieving certain things at school, or perhaps you witnessed a sibling getting into trouble for not achieving and you vowed you would never put yourself in a position like that. The rest of society reinforced how great it was to be an achiever through your school experiences and through media etc.

However it was set up you now have the habitual belief that achievements are a necessary part of your life and you have to achieve. You ARE an achiever! It's part of your identity.

You go through life achieving, achieving, achieving. After leaving school you set yourself up in a job where you were recognised for your achievements, given the accolades you deserved, were rewarded and complimented for your achievements, which validated your worth. You were happy with yourself.

Sure you may have had times of disappointment, but for the most part you usually got what you put your mind to and were able to live up to this identity of being the achiever.

Then it came to having children. All of a sudden you are working harder than you've ever done before, trying to be the perfect parent and going into it with the same expectations – you get whatever you put your mind to... and people will notice you doing it.

Only something's going wrong. It's not working. There are days where you can't get your child to sleep. You don't know what's wrong with them. You don't know what to do. Sometimes you do get it right, but no one cares. You keep the house clean, but no one seems to notice. The kids just mess it up again.

You look around you and you're either failing at something because you've no idea how to handle a situation with your child or you're not feeling very good at being a parent, or on the flip side, you are doing really well at being a parent and no one gives two hoots! It's like you could just disappear off the face of the earth and no one would care.

Subconsciously your mind is comparing. It habitually thinks you should be getting acknowledged for your efforts. Someone should be giving you some credit here! You should be feeling good about this, right?

When you first start to notice that parenting is difficult and you feel like you're not getting many aspects of it right, you go into a bit of a MOOD.

You feel moody for a few hours or a few days here and there, rolling around in your mind how you're not getting anywhere, no one cares and you see loads of evidence to support this thinking. Then the body responds to your thoughts and you feel a bit down, maybe a bit grumpy at the lack of recognition for your efforts.

The fascinating thing about the brain is that when it has its attention on something it starts to look for evidence to back up this train of thought. Ever decided on buying a new car and then all of a sudden you start seeing that same car make and model everywhere? You see ads for it, you see how many people are driving one, and then you hear someone talking about it. You never realised that make and model was so popular. That's because you have your attention on it so your brain goes searching for information to link it to and finds it in your current experiences.

So back to your mood. You begin to find more evidence to support where you have your attention – how you're not able to live up to your identity as the achiever. You begin to see evidence everywhere.

"I can't breastfeed. I can't get my child to stop crying. I can't get the kids to stop fighting. My husband is always cranky at me. I'm always cranky at him. I'm disorganised. I can't seem to string two tasks together. The washing never gets done and if it does, there's just more the next day. I never get any time to myself to do the things I want and I've had enough."

You begin feeling even worse about your life as a parent and the odd hour or day of being moody starts to move into weeks and months of thinking and feeling this way. This process of thinking, feeling, thinking and feeling has now become part of your TEMPERAMENT – an aspect of your personality.

This thinking/feeling loop has started to become a habit – neural connections have formed – and you continue to find even more evidence. Soon enough the months have turned into a year or more and this thinking/feeling loop has become a PERSONALITY TRAIT.

This is where you have come to associate yourself with a new identity.

I AM an angry person. I AM anxious. I AM depressed. I AM miserable. I AM hopeless.

It has become a constant part of who you think you are.

How you think and feel about your life has become a 'state of being'. It's who I AM now.

This is no different to how the achiever identity got set up in the first place. You received the experience of achieving and being acknowledged and rewarded for it over time, and that felt good. It put you in a happy MOOD when people recognised how much you had achieved. After doing this over and over, thinking about how to achieve and feeling good when you did became your temperament. Achieving became an aspect of your personality.

Then as the weeks rolled into years of achieving, getting results, rewards and compliments and feeling good about it, it became a personality trait. 'I AM an achiever' became a 'state of being' and your brain began to associate achievements with your worth – how to pursue pleasure.

But since becoming a parent, this loop of achievement, acknowledgement and reward hasn't happened and despite your efforts to maintain this state of being, you find more and more evidence to support the belief you are failing. The response to this thinking results in you feeling badly about your life. The repetition of this same cycle of thinking and feeling progresses to you now being at the point where depression, anger, resentment or anxiety has become a new 'state of being' that you now use to describe 'who I am'.

You're not having any fun anymore! You don't like who you've become but you don't know how to change it.

Furthermore there is something else going on in the body too. As I mentioned before, every time you have a thought, the brain creates a chemical response which is sent through to the body to tell it what it needs to do, which you recognise either consciously or unconsciously as how you feel.

Because of this constant thinking/feeling loop the cells in your body have adapted to the chemicals these thoughts keep producing. They have literally adjusted themselves to accept the chemical responses as normal. Now they habitually expect you to think this way and thus habitually know how to respond to life's events.

Now the body has become one with the mind. You can feel this way without even having to consciously think about what's going on in your life!

After feeling this way for so long, you might decide it's time to change and you pick up an inspiring book or go to a seminar that teaches you how to change. You begin to try using their principles and thinking.

You start to consciously feed yourself new thoughts about life and try to adapt to your new life as a parent. As a result the brain starts to create new chemical responses, new feelings.

The cells in your body respond in confusion, "What are you doing up there brain? This is not how it works? We don't understand what you're saying. We've adapted to a different way of feeling and we're not sure how to respond to this new chemical you're producing. We don't understand what you're telling us to do. We feel uncomfortable with this unfamiliarity. You better get your act together and correct this".

It sends messages back up to the brain that something is different and the brain begins to correct it by bringing up the old thoughts again that link with the feelings it normally feels. It locates the appropriate beliefs that align with the feelings in the body and starts to search for evidence to support it.

"Don't worry about trying to change. You can't change. You're too set in your ways. Just forget about it. Parenthood is just a miserable time. Look around you. The house is never clean. No one cares whether you are getting anything done or not. The kids don't appreciate you. You're never going to control them. Look at all the evidence you have. You'll never feel differently."

This is a strong force you are reckoning with now and if you let down your conscious guard for a minute, the 'state of being' all comes flooding back to you and restores what has become the body's equilibrium. The new thoughts you were trying to implement from your book or course fall by the wayside. There's just too much evidence to support the old way of thinking.

So back you go, thinking the same, feeling the same and finding more evidence of the same. And nothing changes.

In fact you feel even worse about your achievement identity because now you've just seen even more evidence that you've lost your ability to achieve.

Can you relate to this pattern?

Now you know why it's so difficult to change and why you may not have been successful in the past when you've tried.

You also now know why sometimes you can just feel down for absolutely no obvious reason at all. Subconsciously and physically the thought/feeling loop has been repeated often enough for it to have evolved into your 'state of being'. The cells in your body have even adapted to this loop.

At the beginning of this chapter I asked you a few questions about your lost identity that, now after hearing this explanation, we can answer.

When you say you've lost yourself, what part of yourself do you think you've lost?

It's the part of you that you have learnt to identify as part of your worth – Why I'm valuable to the world and what makes me feel like I'm important and worthy.

It's the learnt 'state of being' that you have habitually come to recognise as I AM.

And why do you need to know who the 'I' is? What purpose does it serve you to know who 'I' am? How does that benefit your life or make things better?

Because knowing who 'I AM' helps me to validate my worth, feel accepted, loved, approved of, acknowledged, cared for, safe, good enough and a part of the world.

When I'm able to feel this way, it makes me feel like my life is okay.

The pursuit of pleasure and the avoidance of pain is ALWAYS the agenda behind the decisions we make and the actions we take.

Your personal identity has become a way in which you have learnt to pursue emotional pleasure – you have become attached to it. Perhaps you are also attached to an idea of how you expected to parent.

The feeling of being lost has arisen because you feel you are no longer able to play these roles in your life due to changing circumstances (i.e. parenthood) and this causes you emotional pain – a feeling of worthlessness.

All of us have our perceptions of our self to contend with, however, what these perceptions are, is really just a set of belief systems – things you have learnt through your life that are the perceived conditions of what defines your worth.

How to change your beliefs.

After reading the explanation of how the brain works and how you've come to attach your worth to your 'I AM' identity, you now understand why you feel the way you do. You may be left wondering how on earth you are going to change it.

Your future happiness may be looking pretty grim right now.

Neuroplasticity.

However, there is another aspect to the human brain that will help you change all this. The term for it is neuroplasticity. This is a term used to describe the brain's ability to change.

In our example, the belief 'I AM an achiever' was set up through repetition, experience and continually engaging in the thinking/feeling loop until it became a part of who 'I AM'.

Then new information was repetitively received, experienced and felt over and over and created the 'I AM depressed' identity or the 'I AM angry/anxious/miserable/lost' identity. That's neuroplasticity in action. Your brain has the ability to change and grow new neural connections in the brain.

With repetition, in our example, the brain grew new pathways to suggest the thinker was now hopeless, a failure, useless, and not able to achieve. This happened, first consciously, then after repeating that thinking/feeling loop over and over until it became a sub-conscious reaction.

This is exactly what you are going to do again to get you back to feeling good about yourself. Except this time you will have the correct information about self-worth and identity so you no longer attach your self-worth to any particular definition of yourself. That way you won't ever feel like you've lost yourself. You'll feel at peace with wherever you are in life.

The reason you haven't changed when you have tried before may be because you have been trying to get back to the point where you are able to live out your pre-parenting identity or another identity you've become attached to which you couldn't play out in your life.

Even if you were re-defining yourself in a healthier

way, perhaps it didn't work because you didn't give it enough time. There wasn't enough repetition, evidence and feelings to create the thinking/feeling loop and the physical neural pathways in the brain didn't get enough time to strengthen.

You see only 5 percent of your brain is conscious. The other 95 percent of your brain is sub-conscious, meaning you're not aware of the processes it is going through. It's only when your thoughts go from your subconscious to your conscious that you become aware of what you are thinking.

This is the bit we're going to work on. In the past you might have tried to change but have just found yourself falling back easily into old habits of thought. That's okay It's normal. Now you understand why this is happening you can be even more vigilant about applying the new way of thinking.

The only way you are going to break any habit is with a new habit. We need to repetitively get into a new thinking/feeling loop. When you do this the old neural pathways (the old thinking) becomes weaker as the new thinking gets stronger. Over time the new thinking becomes the super highway and the old thinking becomes the goat track.

In the brain, a process of synaptic pruning is occurring. To see a visual of real time pruning, find this short one minute video on You Tube – Neural Connections –

Terry Armstrong.*

The funny thing is you already have evidence that you have the ability to change because it's already been done many times in your life. Once upon a time you had felt good about yourself for being able to live up to your perceived identity of self and now you may not feel that way. You already changed your brain.

If you have never felt good about yourself you have still experienced this growing of neural pathways, then weakening of pathways and creation of new ones. When? How about this:

Remember the Santa Claus example?

Do you still believe in Santa Claus or has that belief been upgraded/changed?

Right there is a great example of neuroplasticity in action.

In order to change you need new information about how to identify with yourself in order to create a more peaceful feeling in the body. You need to get involved in a new thinking/feeling loop which is a lot more pleasant.

This is exactly what I dedicate the rest of this book to teaching you.

* http://www.youtube.com/watch?v=8NA_
o1jOjsQ&list=FLLlcjlP8GEMIAfNoX7QpuZQ&index=1

Chapter Two

The Mind TRACK to Happiness Process.

You will find within most of the products at the *Parental Stress Centre* we use a method called the Mind TRACK to Happiness process.

This process is a five step exercise using the acronym of the word TRACK to help you remember which step to take next. Here is what each step stands for:

T – Thoughts

R – Reality

A – Aim

C – Choices, options and solutions

K – Know your plan and action it.

Before we can change something causing stress in our lives we need to understand the original thinking behind the stress.

As you learnt in the evaluation process (see diagram on page 10), what causes you to feel the way you do is how you have evaluated life. We need to understand what we are thinking to make us feel this way before we can change it.

Awareness is 50 percent of change. If we can become aware of those habitual thinking pathways and the associated feeling loop we are already halfway to making a change.

By being aware of a pattern of thinking you begin to observe it. Rather than being involved in that thinking/ feeling loop you have begun to separate yourself from it. You are watching it rather than being caught up in it – the loop cannot continue. You have broken it just by becoming an observer of it.

Once you become aware of your thoughts and habits of thinking the next step is to start consciously feeding your mind new information. The second step of the Mind TRACK to Happiness process is about aligning your thinking with reality.

Beliefs vs Reality.

All stress comes from a conflict between belief and reality. The belief is what you're thinking about the event and what you think it means about you (your self-worth). The reality is what is actually happening and a realistic understanding of life and self-worth.

Right now you have old beliefs about life and self-worth that are in conflict with reality. You are engaging in conversations that are in conflict with reality (I can't be who I used to be. Why can't I just do the things I used to do? etc).

You need to learn a reality based thinking approach to life that will help you accept your life and feel at peace with it. Only from the place of aligning to your reality can you focus on solutions for change.

Think of the five steps on the TRACK process as if you are climbing a ladder.

In the context of your identity issues the bottom of the ladder is how you feel about yourself and your life right now. You may feel lost, lonely, help-less, like a failure, down, critical, judgemental, or any other feeling of emotional pain.

Before you get to the 'what do I do about it' stage, you must first climb the TRACK ladder to understand how you've gotten to where you are and why you are feeling so stressed about your reality. You need to figure out what part of your identity you have attached yourself to and why you feel like you are lost without it.

In the **Thoughts** step we need to identify what you've attached your worth to and how we can change that.

The **Reality** step is where we make some serious changes to your definition of 'you'. This is where we begin to create a new thinking/feeling loop.

From here we move into the **Aim** step of the TRACK process. What do I want? Who do I want to be? This is where you get to redefine yourself, not through any attachments to worth but because you want to experience a particular 'state of being'.

When you understand true self-worth and learn how to accept life's ups and downs without attachment your aims start to become about what you WANT to experience not what you feel like you HAVE TO experience in order to prove yourself.

From this point you get to redesign who you want to be and the sort of experiences you want to experience, including the parent you want to be.

The next step on our ladder is the **Choices** step – how do I get what I want? How do I continue to transform myself into the person I want to be? How do I avoid going back to that identity I attached my worth to?

And then finally we get to the **Know your plan and action it** step. This is where you do what you've learnt in this book. You take action. You begin to create those neural pathways in the brain. You begin to feel differently about your life. You begin to create a new thinking/feeling loop and the cells in your body adapt to a newer, more peaceful environment.

Now you will start to 'BE' the change you desire. Your 'state of being' will become "I AM at peace".

It is likely you came to this book in search of ways to reconnect with who you are, perhaps thinking it would give you advice about how to manage your life better. If you are looking for that I have created *The Parent's Guide to Balance and Getting More You Time*. Which is available from the *Parental Stress Centre* website.

This book is not just about how to define yourself as a person. It goes much deeper. Many people say they want to be happy, but happiness is an emotion we feel. Emotions, as we know, come from how we evaluate life and in order to feel happy we must be evaluating life as going right or meeting our expectations. The reality of life is it doesn't always meet our expectations, so happiness is an elusive goal.

Logically most of us know this, but we still pursue it. What I believe people are really looking for is personal peace. Being able to handle the ups and downs of life without attachment. Being able accept who they are faults and all. And finally, as a parent, to be able to live this peacefulness and teach it to our children.

I want to teach you how to use the Mind TRACK to Happiness process to achieve this goal and right now you already have received the fundamentals to begin this journey.

So are you ready to leave the old you behind and recreate a new sense of peace and happiness?

Let's do this.

Chapter Three

Step One of The Mind TRACK to Happiness Process: Thoughts.

The problem with our habitual thinking is as we become aware of our thoughts we tend to perceive them as truth, dogma, fact or law.

Rule number one in the Thoughts step is, DON'T BELIEVE EVERYTHING YOU THINK!

Remember where your thinking comes from. Your beliefs and thoughts are either a result of how you have perceived past experiences or beliefs from others you adopted because at the time you got enough evidence to be convinced of its truth.

As we become aware of what we are thinking we need to also be aware of the tendency to regard those thoughts as facts and to begin challenging their validity in our current lives.

For example, perhaps your parents used to pick on you for failing your exams or they used to compare you to your academic sibling and now you have taken on the belief you are (I AM) stupid or can't learn.

Or, you were once told you were hopeless at being organised as a teenager and now you have come to believe that 'I AM' an unorganised person.

Or, you were once rewarded for doing something really kind and it felt really good, so now you've taken on a 'be kind to others' identity in order to pursue the same feeling and now you can never say no. You no longer even take pleasure in doing kind acts because now you're doing it because you feel you have to, not because you want to.

Perhaps your current beliefs just don't apply to your current life and circumstances anymore? Perhaps all of your fears, insecurities and current identities come from an old experience you had or an old belief you once adopted that just doesn't have a place in the present?

With awareness, you can start the process of letting them go and moving into the process of unlearning them.

How do I define my personal identity?

As a result of living in the world you have adopted a pretty solid view of who you are, what you expect from yourself and what you think you should do in order to prove your worth.

There are many different labels we have come associate with 'me' so to begin with, let's take a look at the most obvious one – my personal identity.

Personal Identity:

who someone is : the name of a person

: the qualities, beliefs, etc., that make a particular person or group different from others

(Source: Miriam-Webster Dictionary)

Personal Identity is one of the core ways we identify with ourselves. It is the underlying **belief** system that helps you uniquely differentiate yourself from the rest of the world.

Your personal identity consists of traits that uniquely define you as you. There are all of the likes, dislikes, things you do and don't do, personality traits, your abilities and all of your labels and titles (mother, father, teacher, fitness fanatic, perfectionist) that when combined together, mark you as an individual.

Although genetics do play a part in our identity our identities are solidified primarily during the age of zero to seven when the brain is growing its initial neural pathways and learning to understand the world and your role within it. While it can change over time with new experiences it is likely you still identify with yourself in a similar way to how you did in childhood.

Your personal identity began when you were a baby and grew up to play certain roles in your family. Sometimes we are the perfectionist, the 'good girl/boy' the achiever, the peacekeeper. Sometimes we learn to be the best, or the one who never performs well. Both from our experiences and from watching our influencers (primarily our parents) we learn about what we like and don't like and we learn beliefs about how to 'get life right' and what we need to be doing in our lives in order to be living this right life (pleasure) and avoid getting life wrong (pain).

This happens to all of us as human beings. However, it's not actually how we identify our personal selves but why we do it that causes us stress.

It's not the labels or the identity causing us stress, but the self-worth attachment to our identity that can make us feel bad. Believing that only when we live up to certain expectations – activities we do, achievements we must obtain, abilities we must have, labels and judgements we must live up to – do we feel worthy, approved of, loved, accepted, valued or important.

If I can't be who I used to be, how do I validate my worth? How do I seek pleasure (be worthy) and avoid pain (by making my life more valuable) if I can't do things in the way I used to, or if I perceive my new circumstances to be stopping me?

Believing your worth is conditional upon certain expectations, identities or outcomes being met causes your brain to search for evidence of you meeting those conditions. Where does it look? Outside of yourself. You look to others to validate that the conditions of your worth have been met. You look for experiences to confirm you are on the right path in life and if you can't find them you start to believe you are on the wrong path.

The reality is life doesn't always go to plan and everyone's beliefs are different. Other people aren't always going to rate you as meeting the conditions you've set. All of a sudden your worth has become questionable and totally ambiguous.

This line of thought then creates fear.

Maybe I'm not worthy. Maybe I'm not important to the world.

Now your personal identity is not just something you use to describe 'me'. It is now something you NEED to be in order to be worthy. It's something you feel you HAVE to be.

You start to think the answer is to be more, do more or have more in order to feel more (worthy). You go into anxiety mode trying to control situations so you can prove to people that 'I am worthy'.

Look at me, I'm a good parent. I'm intelligent. I know what I'm talking about. I need to get a job. I need to be better at parenting. I need to have a clean house. I need, I need, I need.

Then when you can't control how people perceive you or live up to your identity you start to feel worth-less and down on yourself.

You can then start moving into depression. Or perhaps you continue to swing from depression to anxiety; feeling like a failure one minute and then desperately trying to control life again and get back 'on track' the next.

When our beliefs become about needing to meet specific conditions in order to rate yourself as worthy or good enough, but we are faced with the reality of not fulfilling these roles, we start to feel lost –like you've lost your identity.

What you're really saying is you've lost the ability to prove your worth or validate your existence.

Our personal identity is made up of labels, descriptions and opinions you have that you **believe** sum up who you are and how you prove your individuality (which makes you worthy of being alive).

Attaching self-worth to identity and believing worth is conditional is at the core of society's self-esteem problems and the increase in crime, depression, anxiety and stress.

Wanting to avoid feeling bad is what has brought you to reading this book. However, to stop you feeling this way you don't just need to find your identity, you need a completely different understanding of what truly makes you a valuable person.

Understanding this foundation is going to completely change how you perceive your whole life and what you do with your life from here on in.

Conditional worth means you can only feel good about yourself when life is meeting your expectations so it becomes chance you ever feel good about yourself. I want to help you to change all that so you feel good about yourself from moment to moment.

However, before I get into explaining why you are innately

valuable and helping you to adopt this new unconditional belief about your worth and start feeling more peaceful, I need to teach you to acknowledge and deal with the reality of your judging brain.

The Judging Brain.

We all have a judging brain and we want it to judge. If you had a deadly spider on your shoulder you want your brain to judge this as bad and signal it needs to be removed immediately!

Furthermore your judging brain has been wired to rate you and your life's worth in accordance with beliefs about right and wrong, good and bad, and certain conditions of what is worthy and what is not.

While you won't stop the brain from judging, you can train it to judge life differently. It does take hard work, repetition and consistency in applying new beliefs (which we will call upgrades) and finding evidence to convince the brain not to judge in its habitual way.

Over time, as you continue to upgrade your thinking to a new perception of self-worth (which we will discuss shortly) your brain will begin to habitually learn to think differently about yourself and your role within the world. Remember the term neuroplasticity I discussed in the last chapter?

The attachments you once had to the identity you think you need as a person and as a parent, will dissipate and you will find yourself feeling relaxed, inspired and motivated by life in a way you've never known before. You will find joy in the simplest of moments.

Getting to know yourself.

The first step on the Mind TRACK to happiness process is to understand your thinking. In the context of finding your lost identity you need to become aware of how you are currently identifying with yourself and what part of yourself you have attached your self-worth to.

Filling out the following questionnaire is going to give you an overview of your beliefs surrounding yourself and how those beliefs were set up. As we've been discussing, most of the beliefs you are evaluating your life with were set up in childhood.

Your answers to the questionnaire are going to help you to identify the specific beliefs that are causing your stress and where they were adopted from (which parent or what experiences caused you to be convinced of their truth).

From here you will be able to recognise a pattern in your thinking and it will become quite obvious how this thinking is contributing to the feelings you have about your life.

This questionnaire is just for you so please be completely honest in your answers. Your brain will know how to link to the answers that are relevant to the question.

Try not to screen answers or give them loads of thought. Just go with whatever comes up first regardless of whether you like it or not. Be as detailed as possible, the more information you give the more effective the next exercise will be.

Exercise One
What identity am I attached to and where did I learn to attach it to my self-worth?

Instructions: Complete the following questionnaire.

Section One: Your childhood family

How would you describe your family (from childhood) – siblings, parents etc.

_____
_____
_____

How would you describe your interactions with each other?

_____
_____
_____

Were there many conflicts in the family and how were they handled?

_____
_____
_____

Was there an event from your childhood that you still remember often (good or bad)?

_____

_____

_____

What was your role in the family? What did that role require you to do?

(Note: everyone has a specific role they played, such as youngest, smartest, or prettiest.)

_____

_____

_____

Are you still playing that role today?

_____

_____

_____

Was religion a part of your life?

- If yes which one?
- Does it have a part in your life today and how?

_____

_____

_____

What is your family's cultural back ground? Does this, and has this, affected your life?

If so, how?

_____

_____

_____

Section Two – Yourself

How would you describe yourself?

_____

_____

_____

What are some of the specific beliefs you remember being taught about:

Yourself:

_____

_____

Family:

_____

_____

Women:

_____

_____

Men:

_____

_____

Children:

_____

_____

Achievements:

_____

_____

Money:

_____

_____

Marriages/Relationship:

_____

_____

What are the issues you think really cause your stress or loss of identity?

_____

_____

_____

Do you think your life is going wrong? Why or why not?

_____

_____

_____

Are you happy with your life right now? Why or why not?

_____

_____

_____

What is needed in order to fix your life or make it better?

_____

_____

_____

Why can't you accept your life right now?

_____

_____

_____

What aspect of yourself do you hold in high regard (that is – what do you like about yourself?)

_____

_____

_____

What aspects of yourself do you hold in low regard (that is – what don't you like about yourself)?

_____

_____

_____

What characteristics do you feel have been lost from your identity?

_____

_____

_____

What do you think you need in order to rediscover your identity?

_____

_____

_____

Why do you want to be the person that you used to be?

_____

_____

_____

Section Three – Your Mother

(or female primary caregiver. If your mother was absent during your childhood, please proceed with the questions, as you will still hold beliefs about your mother. If you had both a mother who was absent and another primary female caregiver, please complete the questionnaire for each person.)

Describe your mother

_____

_____

_____

What do you think she liked about herself?

_____

_____

_____

What do you think she liked about you?

_____

_____

_____

What do you think she disliked about herself?

_____

_____

_____

47

What do you think she needed in order for her life to be successful?

_____

_____

_____

What do you think she felt you needed in order for your life to be successful?

_____

_____

_____

Was there an event that occurred as a child between your mother and yourself that still impacts you today?

_____

_____

_____

Name two lessons you learnt from your mother?

What you would use today?

_____

_____

_____

What you wouldn't use today?

_____

_____

_____

Section Four – Your Father

(or male primary caregiver. If your father was absent during your childhood, please proceed with the questions, as you will still hold beliefs about your father. If you had both a father who was absent and another primary male caregiver, please complete the questionnaire for each person.)

Describe your father

_____

_____

_____

What do you think he liked about himself?

_____

_____

_____

What do you think he liked about you?

_____

_____

_____

What do you think he disliked about himself?

_____

_____

_____

What do you think he needed in order for his life to be successful?

_____

_____

_____

What do you think he felt you needed in order for your life to be successful?

_____

_____

_____

Was there an event that occurred as a child between your father and yourself that still impacts you today?

_____

_____

_____

Name two lessons you learnt from your father?

What you would use today?

_____

_____

_____

What you wouldn't use today?

_____

_____

_____

Part B

Use the following questions to help ascertain the pattern of thinking that highlights what part of your identity you have your self-worth attached to.

Sometimes it's not until we look back at our answers that we gain an overall view of the beliefs that lie in our minds and how they are contributing to your stress.

- Are there are repetitive words you used within your questionnaire?

- Were there any repetitive themes? (For example, I kept referring to ideas around achievement, or I found that I kept saying I should be doing more to stop something).

- Can you see any similarities between one of your parents and your own character and behaviours?

- Was there something that you needed to do in order to win the approval of your parents or to feel accepted, loved, important, approved of, or good enough in the eyes of one or both of your parents?

- Did you observe a sibling experiencing emotional pain due to a certain behaviour and you become the opposite of that sibling's behaviour (a subconscious approach to avoiding emotional pain)?

- Were there any ideas about how a life 'should' be lived and how yours is going wrong?

- From your answers to this questionnaire, can you see where you have attached your identity to your self-worth? What have you learnt about yourself from doing this exercise?

_____

_____

_____

_____

_____

Recognising my child-self.

As a result of this questionnaire I hope you have gained a tremendous amount of insight into why you feel the way you do and how your beliefs about yourself have been set up from your childhood and your life experiences to date.

For example, you may have realised just how often you mentioned achievements as being a focus in your childhood, or just how often you had to play the role of pleasing others, or taking care of others and you recognise you still feel like you have to play that role today.

Perhaps you identified with being put down over and over again, or wore the brunt of anger, criticisms or harsh judgements and you have learnt to define yourself in that way.

Perhaps there was a cultural or family value system drilled into you and now you are holding onto the belief life can only go right when you are living up to that expectation. When you aren't able to meet that expectation you feel lost, down, depressed or anxious.

From the answers you gave in your questionnaire there will be a pattern to your thinking that will highlight the specific beliefs behind your stress and the attachments to your self-worth.

Whatever pattern you establish it is important to be able to understand that these beliefs were adopted at a time when you were naïve about life as a child and didn't know any different. As children we don't have any other reference point. Through observation, self-experience and being convinced by those we trusted we took on these beliefs as truths.

It is our natural human instinct to pursue pleasure and avoid pain so as a child you learnt how to pursue emotional pleasure through receiving whatever love, approval, attention, acceptance or acknowledgement you could get by playing the roles you did. And now as an adult you are still playing those roles in order to feel good (pursue pleasure) or be worthy.

When you look at those beliefs within the context of your logical adult mind you may find they are no longer relevant. Because those beliefs are physical neural connections in the brain they aren't going to go away with ease.

To help you to begin disassociating with the beliefs you found in your questionnaire it is often helpful to name your past identity, like it was another person separate to you. I name mine 'Lizzy'. Whenever I catch myself thinking in the repetitive way I do, which is to doubt myself, put myself down and speak harshly to myself, I recognise that voice as being Lizzy.

Lizzy is just my child-self who learnt to speak badly to herself because she believed she had to maintain her golden child status in order to be better than her sister. Her sister used to get in trouble a lot for failing exams or not working hard enough in our family shop, so Lizzy learnt in order to avoid the emotional pain of experiencing the rejection she perceived her sister to be getting she needed to do better, be better and achieve more things.

Lizzy was acknowledged for her achievements which further validated her worth being connected to her achievements. Whenever she found she was not achieving or hadn't received any acknowledgements for a while, she began to berate herself and judge herself harshly.

Of course Lizzy is me, but the way I have learnt to disassociate with those incorrect, past indoctrinated beliefs is to lump them together as a child identity who adopted this way of thinking at a time when she didn't know any better.

Think of a child you know between the ages of zero to seven – one of your own children perhaps – and you will get a sense of just how naïve they are to the understandings of life. You get a sense of how easily they can adopt incorrect views and beliefs about life and their self-worth.

That was you too as a child and all of the beliefs causing you stress right now are just your child-self thinking in that same naïve way.

Your thinking about yourself is habitual (physical neural connections residing in your subconscious). They are there because of the repetition and consistency of evidence that supported them to be perceived truths. This evidence came from your experiences. How could you possibly have different habitual thoughts? How could you have possibly learnt to believe something different with the experiences you have had?

Naming and recognising that child-self whenever those thoughts arise helps you to be more understanding of their nature. You may even become compassionate toward this part of yourself and the way he/she felt when growing up.

If you heard one of your children speaking to themselves in the same way you speak to yourself, or you realised they were feeling so badly about themselves, how would you react to them? Would you berate them further? Would you say that they were stupid, useless, hopeless or an idiot for thinking that way?

Or would you want to educate them to think differently about life? Would you want to show them evidence of why those beliefs were not true?

Because this is what we need to do for your child-self. You need to give this child an education and show them evidence that their old way of thinking is not true.

Exercise Two
Naming my identity.

From the pattern of thinking you discovered in exercise one, name your child self and describe his/her personality traits and his/her beliefs about life and self-worth.

As you go about your day start to notice just how often you are perceiving life through this child-self and practice recognising these thoughts as an identity (who now has a name) who was naïve and didn't know any better, and who just needs an education on how to think differently.

Chapter Four

Step Two of the Mind TRACK to Happiness Process: Reality.

In order for you to stop the thinking/feeling loop currently causing you to feel bad your brain needs new information, new beliefs and evidence to reinforce new truths.

This will occur through observation, self-experience and being convinced of these new beliefs.

Within this book I hope to be the convincer of these new beliefs. I will present the new information and attempt to show you evidence of its truth so it will resonate with you and you will believe me.

The observation part and the self-experience part will be up to you. Without those two components you are only reading information. It will be the application of information you read in the next four steps of the Mind TRACK process that will create changes in your life.

Have you ever heard of the saying "you can lead a horse to water, but you can't make it drink"? The same applies to changing your thinking.

You can read all of the self-help material and do all of the self-improvement courses in the world, but if you don't apply the information you are learning and make an effort to consciously think differently you won't bring about change.

We know 5 percent of the brain function is conscious and 95 percent is subconscious. This is why awareness of your thinking from step one is just as important as the rest of these steps.

The 95 percent holds the old stress causing habitual thinking. Once you become aware of that thinking you switch to the conscious 5 percent. You must use the conscious mind to replace those old thoughts with new information. Over time and with the repetitive evidence from observation, self-experience and being convinced, your subconscious will learn how to think this new way more habitually. This is neuroplasticity in action.

With that said, let me show you how you can change your thinking.

Accepting the reality of the small picture.

Whenever you are feeling stressed you will be rolling around in a story about how life should be different to what you're experiencing, how you are missing out on the way things should be, how you or someone else should be doing more, or doing something else and because of this unwanted situation you rate your life as having decreased in value.

This is the small picture and this story is in conflict with reality. The reality is you are where you are. You're not somewhere else. You aren't living another life, or the life you used to have. The reality is what is presently here in front of you right now. We have to accept this reality in order to begin the process of feeling differently about it.

You don't have to like your reality, but you do need to accept it is here for now. We will work on how to change your reality as you move through the Mind TRACK to Happiness process. The first part of this reality step is being able to say to yourself: "the reality is [fill in the blank]".

You are a parent. Your child is at a certain stage in their personal development. They are learning, just like you are. You are at a particular stage in your personal development too, as is your partner, friends and other family members.

If you are experiencing difficulties in the area of parenting – perhaps with breastfeeding, or getting your child to sleep, or your child's backchat, or not getting enough time out, or feeling like you have too much workload – it is irrelevant how you got to that place. The reality is you are here now.

It is very difficult to get to the Aim, Choices and Know your plan and action it steps of the Mind TRACK to Happiness process when you are still rolling around in a story about how your life should be different.

One of the most powerful statements my husband taught me to say to myself whenever I catch myself engaging in this kind of thinking is: "Jackie, you are in conflict with reality." This statement is usually enough to bring my attention back into the present moment so I can move onto finding solutions.

You can't get clean by rolling in the mud! So we have to align our thinking with the reality of where you are in your life to date.

Once you have brought your attention back to the reality of your situation you then need to help the brain learn another way to think about your present reality so you aren't feeling so stressed or emotional about it.

Three new perspectives to change the way you feel about your life.

When you attach your self-worth to the 'right' life you think you are supposed to be having you are immediately in conflict with reality and will feel stress.

You believe this current situation means something negative about you or your whole life. Somehow your life has become less valuable, worth less or isn't as important or meaningful as it is supposed to be. The attachment between your beliefs about the 'right' life with your self-worth (or life's worth) is what is causing you to feel these emotions.

We now know where those beliefs came from (your childhood) and you are able to name the child-self who came to believe those things.

Now we need to retrain that child-self to hold a completely different outlook on your unwanted events and situations.

The following three perspectives of life will change the way you perceive your world. Once you accept the reality of where you are you can move on to being solution focussed about what to do about your present situation. These three perspectives will enable you to let go of your attachments to this 'right life' you believe you should be living.

New perspective #1: Life is a story of ups and downs.

This first new perspective will expand your viewpoint out to the bigger picture of what your current reality actually means about your life (as opposed to what you believe your current reality means about you).

We get stressed because we attach ourselves to the life we used to have. We attach ourselves to wanting someone else's life because we think they have it better and we believe we should be having that life instead of the one we're having.

In our minds we are trying to live a life that is imagined and is perceived as being right, but is in direct conflict with our reality.

This is because we have a brain that judges using information cemented from our past experiences. It habitually gets stuck in a picture of how it used to be or how we want it to be. It appears everyone else is getting life right but you are not. However, you are only seeing things through one narrow minded perspective (the small picture) and it's not an accurate one.

You need to train your mind to bring its attention into the current moment and broaden your perspective so you can see that none of us spend our lives on a direct pathway to success. Life is a story that comprises of ups and downs.

We all live in a world of polarity.

Where there is an in, there is always an out. Where there is a north, there is a south. Where there is an up, there is a down. Where there is a high, there is a low. The polarity exists in your life too because everything you experience in life also has its ups and downs. Your relationships, work, schooling, friendships, money, even parenting.

Sometimes we get what we want. Other times we don't. Events come and go. Life changes from what it was before. New experiences come into our lives and go again and as human beings we learn, grow and change.

As a parent your life has changed. Like I said before, parenthood changes you on every level – physically, mentally, emotionally, morally and ethically. You aren't the same person you were before.

To be able to let go of the attachment to your idea of a 'right' life you need to learn how to accept where you are in your life right now and be able to see the highs also occurring in your current life, not just the lows.

Remember the brain looks for evidence of what you put your attention on and it may be habitually looking for evidence of how your life is not meeting the standards you believe define your worth. To change this habit you need to consciously (with the 5 percent) search for a different way to see life.

To avoid stress you need to move with the tides of your changing life and accept the reality of the highs and lows without attachment. Look for evidence of both of the polar opposites in your life. Recognise where there is a down there is always a subsequent or a preceding high.

When you are in your narrow minded viewpoint that life is going wrong you tend to think you are the only one experiencing hardships and guess what evidence the mind finds to support that perspective? All the evidence of how everyone else has got it right and you haven't.

It may be true that life isn't unfolding in the way you would like it to right now, but this isn't an indication that life is going wrong or that your life is worse than anyone else's. It's just an experience you are having in life right now that's different to the one you expected.

Everybody experiences ups and downs. No one is exempt from this reality. It might just be they are experiencing difficulties in a different area to you at a different stage in their life story and you don't know about it. Or you have your attention so attached to how your life is going wrong and how bad your life is that you are not seeing any evidence of their hardships. You're not seeing the full picture.

There are always highs and lows going on in everyone's life. You need to consciously train the brain to remember this reality and look for evidence of both ends of the scale so you are always looking at the whole picture.

When you are stressed or emotional you tend to catastrophise events by only seeing what's going wrong. You rate one or several low events as meaning your life is going wrong and you stop taking notice of all the things that are going right.

Exercise Three
Evidence of your life having highs AND lows.

Part A
Create a time line of your life. You may decide to do the last 12 months, two years or the entirety of your life.

Make your time line a wave line to illustrate the ups and downs that have occurred in your life. Try to recall as many events as you can where you were enjoying your experiences (highs) and not enjoying your experiences (lows). Do this with as many different categories of your life (parenting, relationships, work, friendships, social activities, money etc.).

Look for evidence of how your life isn't always going wrong, nor is it always going right. It's just a series of ups and downs and experiences you have had.

When you've finished this exercise take a moment to reflect on what you are seeing in front of you. This is your unique and special life story, complete with highs and lows, just like everyone else.

Part B

Choose someone in your life who you know well and who you think has their life going right. Contemplate the events that have occurred in their life. Has their life always been smooth sailing? Have they ever struggled with something, gone through a hard time, or suffered adversity? Have they ever felt insecure about something or failed before they got successful? Have they ever made mistakes or felt emotional or stressed?

Think about as many highs you can remember from their life, as well as the lows that have occurred so you can see that they too have experienced some challenges. It's not just exclusive to you.

There is no right way for life to unfold. Even if you can't subscribe to this notion at this stage, you can at least acknowledge the reality that you don't always live the perceived 'right' way all the time.

If your life is going wrong because of some unwanted events, then everyone's life is going wrong, because we all experience highs and lows, just in different ways.

When you can see this reflected in your own life story (see evidence), you tend to be able to accept the difficult times more freely because you are no longer catastrophising this current experience as meaning you are having a wrong life. It just becomes an unenjoyable experience you're having right now nestled amongst the highs and lows that make up your life story.

The next new perspective will help you to go one step further where you are able to see the value in the unwanted experience.

New Perspective #2: Everything has value.

Being able to see the value in your current situation is another crucial skill to help you feel differently about your difficult times.

The new perspective – *everything has value* – reminds you to move your attention away from what you're not getting in your life and onto what you are getting.

Even though you may not be experiencing the life you think you should have, you are still experiencing a life full of experiences that will be adding benefit to your life. You just need to learn how to see the benefit.

It's what I call, finding the hidden good in the bad.

You can find this hidden good by searching for evidence of how you are learning from this event, improving (yourself) because of this event or seeing how this event might lead to something you wanted.

Learning from an event.

Often as parents we belittle ourselves for not knowing how to do something. Perhaps you went on an outing with your kids and forgot to pack snacks. Having experienced the low of having to listen to your children complain they are hungry all day you ended up resorting to takeaway foods. You just learnt that next time you need to pack snacks. You wouldn't have learnt that if you hadn't experienced the low of hearing the complaints and feeling bad for giving them takeaway food.

You just received an experiential lesson from an unwanted event.

Here's another example that happened to me.

Perhaps you became aware that yelling at your children was becoming a habit that you didn't like, yet you still continued to do it. One particular day you just happened to catch the look of fear on your child's face when you did it and all of a sudden you realised the full extent of what you were doing to your child. Aside of the usual beating-up of one's self, the value comes from the fact this now prompts you to get help. It woke you up and reminded you this isn't the way you want to parent.

Perhaps it led you to the *Parental Stress Centre*, or to talk to you doctor or to ask your friends or family for advice. Perhaps it got you to seek information about how to do things differently and cope better.

None of these things would have happened if you didn't have that unwanted episode between you and your child.

That's not to say we want things like this to occur in our lives. We never want to experience these unwanted events – that's why they are unwanted. However, they do occur because the reality is we all experience ups and downs, and there is value because they teach us how to 'do' something, or how to do it better.

Improving myself because of this event.

Often our unwanted experiences are wake up calls – experiences that highlight where we need to learn and grow as a human being.

I guess you could say these times present us with platforms to spiritually improve. Those times when you are feeling at your lowest, experiencing extreme hardships and your self-worth plummets. These are often the times when you have no choice but to change.

Have you ever experienced something unwanted and then said to yourself it was the best thing that ever happened to you because of what it taught you?

Our unwanted moments are our gifts, the very experiences we need to lift us to another level of being in this life.

The feelings you were experiencing before reading this book have been valuable because they forced you to buy this book and learn a different approach to life. That experience is part of you learning and growing in the area of self-improvement and personal development. This is what we do in life.

Furthermore, when you get these lessons in life what do you think you do with them? You use them to change how you feel and you share them with other people. You teach your children about the lessons you've learnt or how to avoid experiencing what you did. You speak to friends, family and sometimes even strangers about your experiences and how you moved through them, thus teaching them too.

Even when you haven't consciously learnt from your experience yet, you still share that information with people and they learn something about their lives from your adversity. Have you ever felt grateful for your own life after hearing someone else's tragic story?

Every event has value – for you and for those around you. The purpose of life is to live, learn, grow, share and evolve.

When you experience some of the worst lows in your life they are usually the biggest indicators that you need to drastically change something in your character, or the experience automatically changes the very core of who you are. This change leads you to a more meaningful life.

These times are what I call life learning – they propel us to another level of human existence and force us to learn more about ourselves.

This unwanted event led me to something wanted or enjoyable.

What if as a result of yelling at your child and getting your wake-up call to change you found a parenting forum or a community group that ended up becoming a lot more than just help for your anger?

What if you met your best friend or your life partner because of an unwanted event? What if because of a tragedy you experienced directly or indirectly you had to redesign your whole life and re-prioritise what was important to you?

The September 11 incident in America where the planes were overtaken by terrorists and flown into the twin towers did this for a lot of people. Should it have happened? No. But the reality is that it did. It was an unwanted event. We can continue to get upset over how it was wrong and how people are now missing out on their 'right' life (having their loved ones still with them), however this viewpoint will only keep us stuck in emotional stress.

Once again, you would only be looking at the low perspective and not the polar opposite of the highs that also come from our events.

There were so many stories that came from this incident from all over the world that were so valuable to human existence and to the individuals benefiting from the value.

- Security was stepped up all over the world, thus preventing this from happening elsewhere, or as often.

- People who were working 60–70 hour weeks realised how precious life was and totally changed their lifestyles.

- People reconciled with loved ones who they had fought with for years over trivial issues because they realised that holding onto animosity isn't worth it.

- Communities rallied together to help one another, where before they couldn't care less about each other.

- Friendships and bonds were formed between the fire fighters, police officers and volunteers who were directly or indirectly involved in the incident.

- Even those who experienced the loss of a loved one from the tragedy have had to learn how to move on and build resilience. It made them stronger or led them to have other enjoyable relationships, either by eventually meeting new partners, or growing closer to other family members.

While we would never wish those tragedies on anyone, unenjoyable and low experiences happen to everyone and they always provide some value to our lives in some way. They always lead to another high and another low in one way or another.

By finding the value in your unwanted events, you are not saying you wanted that event to happen. You are just aligning with the reality that life is full of ups and downs. You are acknowledging that unwanted events teach you something to help you experience other events and all of the highs are linked to the lows and all of the lows are linked to the highs. You don't experience one without the other.

Your life is just a series of experiences that lead to more experiences and they are all just part of your overall experience of life – your life's story. Life can never go wrong. It just goes differently then you thought it would.

Exercise Four
Find the hidden good in the bad.

Part A
Take another look at your time line from exercise three on page 63. Choose a couple of lows from your time line and try to find the hidden good in the bad. Look for:

- What did you learn from the event – how to do something or how to do it better?

- How did this event force you, or encourage you, to improve on yourself or make changes to improve the circumstances of your life?

- Did this event lead to another wanted or enjoyable experience that couldn't have happened if your low hadn't happened?

Part B

Think about your life right now and what you are perceiving as being wrong or unwanted in your current reality. Try to find the hidden good in the bad:

- What are you learning from this situation – how to do something or how to do it better?

- Is this event a wake-up call to improve yourself or encourage you to change the conditions of your life?

- Has this event already led to you another experience that was enjoyable or beneficial to you?

You may need to think really hard about this exercise, but if you continue to search for evidence of the hidden good in the bad, your brain will find it, because that is where you have your attention.

Every time you catch your child-self going back to that habit of looking for evidence of what you are missing out on bring your attention back to finding what the value of this moment is – what you are getting.

You can even start a gratitude journal where you list 15 things per day you are grateful for. Find five items from each of the three elements – something I'm learning, an area I've improved upon in myself today and something wanted that is occurring in my life.

If you do this for two weeks straight, you will feel amazing. Trust me, I've done it before. This exercise alone can completely change the way you feel about your life.

New perspective #3 – My life is ALWAYS valuable. I am always 100% worthy.

This final new perspective that will help you to feel differently about yourself and your life is probably the most important of the three perspectives to get your head around.

The fundamental reason you are feeling stressed or emotional is because you have rated your current circumstances as meaning something negative about your current life or your self-worth.

Being able to recognise that your life is full of ups and downs, it isn't going wrong and then being able to find the hidden good in the bad will help you to feel differently about how your life is unfolding. It helps you to broaden your perspective to the bigger picture.

However it may not be helping you to feel better about yourself as a person, as a parent or as an individual.

You may still feel lost about where your place is in the world and are struggling to adjust to your new roles in life after big changes occur and the letting go of the roles you left behind.

We get attached to all the definitions of self we hold onto as proving we are worthy or important. You became aware of some of these attachments in the questionnaire you completed in exercise one on page 41.

In addition to attachments to our personal identity we also have other ways we describe our worth. We talk about having a healthy self-image, improving our self-confidence, learning to have self-respect and raising our self-esteem. When we are feeling badly about ourselves, we turn to these terms and seek help in improving these areas of our life.

However all of them rely on life matching your conditioned beliefs and on seeking evidence from outside of yourself to prove your worth, rather than simply knowing you are always unconditionally valuable.

Let me show you what I mean:

Self-Image:

> *The way you think about yourself and*
> *your abilities or appearance*

(Source: Miriam-Webster Dictionary)

How do I appear to the world? What image do I need to live up to so I can be assessed as being worthy to the world? These are the questions we ask when looking at our self-image.

You have a pre-conceived idea (a **belief**) that has been formed through your experiences of life about how one is 'supposed' to appear to the world in order to be rated as worthy. If you believe you meet that ideal you will feel like you have a healthy self-image. If you do not believe you meet that ideal, you probably won't have a healthy self-image.

But is self-image an accurate way to define your worth? Who defines whether your image is appropriate or not and how is that definition validated?

If you believe a good image of a mum is one who breastfeeds until the age of two years old, who is it that validates that image as being correct? Won't that differ depending on beliefs? Won't others rate your image of a mum depending on *their* beliefs?

Even if you don't care what other people think or believe if you have attached your worth as a good mum to being able to breastfeed until your child is two and you can't (for example if you weren't able to breastfeed any longer) your self-image has just been compromised, leaving you feeling bad again.

If you used to believe your self-image was heavily identified as a 'successful working woman/man' before children and you gave up work to be a stay at home parent, then perhaps you don't know where you fit in anymore – your self-image may have taken a beating.

Or perhaps you were an attractive, slim, well dressed woman before having children and used to get loads of attention and acknowledgements from others about how you looked. But since having children you now feel like a tired, frumpy woman that no one looks twice at. This can be something else that can play havoc with your self-image beliefs.

Working towards improving your self-image will likely result in you only feeling worthy when you are perceived by others as meeting your ideal of self or when you believe you are matching the way you think you should look to the world .

Self-Confidence:

Confidence in oneself and in one's powers and abilities.

(Source: Miriam-Webster Dictionary)

Am I sure of myself? Do I think I'm doing the right thing? How able am I?

Your level of self-confidence will vary depending on how you rate what you are doing and how well you think you are doing it. At one end of the confidence spectrum you will believe you are doing something right and are good at it. At the other end you will fear you are not good at something or can't do it right. In between will be your level of confidence.

The reality is your abilities fluctuate within different areas of your life within different times. But self-confidence relies on believing in your abilities so you are likely to only feel confident when you are getting life right again (or doing life the way you think you should).

For example, you might be super confident in a work

scenario, but as a parent you feel like you have no idea what you are doing and are riddled with doubt.

Having self-confidence still doesn't always make you feel good about yourself because you are still relying on conditional beliefs and judgements to validate whether you are okay or not.

Understanding true self-worth will automatically increase your overall self-confidence. It won't necessarily make you better at something if the reality is you are not well practiced at something (like breastfeeding for example). However, you will be confident in your understanding that it's okay to learn. You will accept the reality that you are not going to be good at all things at all times. Those attachments to *needing* to be good at things will disappear when you are in touch with the knowledge of true self-worth.

Self-Respect:

> **A proper respect for oneself as a human being.**
>
> *Regard for one's own standing or position.*

(Source: Miriam-Webster Dictionary)

What do I deserve?

Again, this will be answered in accordance with what you believe about your conditional worth. If you believe you don't meet the conditions of worth and you rate yourself as being worth-less, then you probably won't be too surprised when other people treat you as worth-less too.

"Typical. That always happens to me."

The word respect basically means; "I expect you to treat me the way I believe I should be treated." You teach people how to treat you. If you have a low opinion of yourself you are likely to teach people (mostly subconsciously) to treat you in a disrespectful way.

This is especially true when you've grown up with people constantly belittling you, hurting you (emotionally or physically) or treating you in a disrespectful way. It becomes an expected response whenever you deal with other people. You've never known it to be any different, so how would you know how to teach people to treat you any different?

The habitual mind gets used to this response from people. In fact it even searches for ways to keep it going, because that is its norm. Because you've been exposed to it your whole life, at some level your brain thinks you deserve this treatment. You've been taught to believe it and guess what evidence your brain finds to support these beliefs?

Logically you know you deserve to be treated with respect, but logic isn't running your life most of the time. Logic is a conscious (5 percent) function of the brain. The habitual beliefs about life (the 95 percent subconscious) is running the show from the background.

On the flip side if you have a high self-respect it means

you believe you do deserve a higher level of treatment. You believe you meet the conditions of your worth (at least in this moment of my life) and expect others to treat you as such. This is where you want to be in life.

However, sometimes this too can cause problems if you become attached to *needing* other people to validate your worth and rely on them treating you with respect in order to continue to feel good. Reality is that people are going to behave in accordance with their beliefs, not yours, and they won't always rate you in the same regard as you rate yourself. They therefore won't always treat you the way you think you should be treated.

While self-respect is a trait we all need to learn and develop it still is not an accurate representation of your uncompromisable 100 percent worth because it still relies on you believing that you are good enough to be treated in a kind way.

Self-Esteem:

Respect for or a favourable opinion of oneself.

An unduly high opinion of oneself; vanity.

(Source: Collins English Dictionary)

Opinion – that word says it all. A belief you have about something is an opinion. Beliefs are learnt. We are conditioned to believe certain things about ourselves and our place in the world.

Esteem actually means 'to rate'. Our self-esteem is our rating of our self and it fluctuates according to how you are perceiving life and your role you play within the current events of your life.

As a parent you are rating yourself right now. Am I rating that I meet that conditions of a good (worthy) parent?

When you get your life right and have success over something you rate yourself as worth more. You have a value attachment to your success.

'I'm proud of myself'. 'I feel awesome'. 'Finally life is starting to be good again'. 'Look at me go. I'm on fire now!'

But when life goes wrong, you can equally have a value judgement on that too

'I've failed'. 'I've stuffed my life up'. 'I'm such an idiot/ loser.' 'I've completely lost the plot'. 'I don't know who I am anymore'.

If life doesn't meet the conditions you have learnt defines your worth you feel bad, but when it does meet those conditions you feel good.

That means feeling good about yourself relies on situations matching your beliefs on how life should unfold. The reality is life doesn't always match your beliefs. Feeling good is a game of chance because now only when you can get life right can you feel worthy.

Now you have learnt the incorrect belief that underlies all stress, depression, anxiety and subsequently undesirable behaviours like crimes, nastiness and a lack of love – the belief that your worth is conditional.

Anxiety comes from trying to control being seen as good enough and fearing you won't be able to prove yourself as good enough. Depression is where you believe you've failed at being good enough and don't want to participate in life for fear of being even more of a failure. Anger is when you feel like you have lost the power to prove you are good enough and is an attempt to regain your power back again. Guilt is where you regret having done something that compromises your worthiness.

And this all comes from your beliefs about how to rate yourself. It comes from your self-esteem – how well you rate yourself according to your beliefs.

Think of a judgement you regularly have on yourself. Does it apply to everyone? Is your best friend worth-less when they don't live up to that same expectation? If this judgement doesn't apply to everyone then it can't be reality. If your rating of yourself can differ in opinions from one person to another it is not reality, it is just a belief.

Reality is factual. It cannot be disputed. Reality means you will not find evidence of it being any other way.

Reality is you are as tall as you are. Reality is that you weigh what you weigh. Reality is right now you are at where you are at in your life. Reality is everyone has their ups and downs. Reality is there is value in everything because you are always learning, improving yourself and needing the unwanted in order to get to the wanted.

Your life is always valuable.

The reality is your life is always valuable and 100 percent worthy. I haven't yet convinced you of that yet, have I? The jury's still out on that one.

These self-worth descriptions – self-image, self-confidence, self-respect and self-esteem – all attempt to describe your value. However, they don't even come close to describing your real value because they are all conditioned upon beliefs and beliefs are not always reliable representations of truth.

Personal identity relies on labels, definitions of yourself and character traits you feel you have to live up to.

Self-image relies on beliefs you have about how you should appear to the world.

Self-confidence relies on beliefs about whether you are good enough at an ability.

Self-respect relies on beliefs about how you deserve to be treated based on how you rate yourself.

Self-esteem relies on beliefs that rate whether you're getting life right or not and your rating of how worthy you are.

If you've grown up with conditioning to believe you are hopeless, useless and a good for nothing so and so, do you think you're going to be able to find evidence of your worth in any of these descriptions of value?

It's likely you will just find more evidence of the same – I'm not good enough – or you just pin your worth on another label or set of expectations of yourself that are still conditional.

Even if you had a great upbringing, if you have attached your value to an identity, a way of being, an expectation, an outcome or an ability, do you think you're always going to be able to feel good about yourself at all times either?

Working on self-image, self-confidence, self-respect and self-esteem are all valuable exercises. There's no disputing that. However, we must realise these descriptions are judgement based and will fluctuate according to how you are perceiving life in each moment.

The bigger picture is that none of these terms are an accurate representation of your true self-worth. In fact, even the dictionary definition of self-worth doesn't even describe it accurately.

Self-worth:

Respect for or a favourable opinion of oneself.

(Source: Collins English Dictionary)

Even this description alludes to the idea of your worth being rated via your opinions. It's still conditional upon belief.

If even the dictionary doesn't get it right, what hope do we have of understanding true worth?

I believe a more appropriate definition of self-worth would be:

> *Self-worth: a true understanding of one's*
> *worth / value to the world.*

Truth is reality. Reality is factual and cannot be disputed.

The reality of self-worth is an understanding that your life is always valuable.

You are always 100 percent worthy.

Now it's likely there may be a side of you that reads this definition of worth and may be feeling slightly uncomfortable with that statement. Perhaps you want to believe, but fail to see how it could be true. This is just your self-esteem (your rating system) causing you to react this way.

The brain judges and it wants to compare that statement with what you believe. It is looking for evidence of whether this new information is true. All it can come up with is that your worth is conditional and you may not be meeting those conditions. It doesn't understand that statement and asks, *"How can that statement be true? We have evidence to suggest you aren't worthy because you aren't doing x, y and z."*

However, it's only because you don't yet have enough evidence to convince you this statement is true.

So let me give you that evidence.

You are 100 percent worthy right now because you are you. By being you with the information you have, the strengths, the weaknesses, the beliefs, the actions, reactions, decisions, likes, dislikes, appearances, choice of clothing, job you do and every other part of who you are, you are living life and always influencing the lives of other people around you.

Because of other people's experience of you just as you are they are learning, making decisions, taking action, establishing what their likes and dislikes are, establishing strengths and weaknesses, and having experiences of life.

Every single person on this planet plays a vital role to the contribution of life in their own unique ways. We have been conditioned to believe that life has to be this big grand publicly important existence or that we need to be doing something meaningful or specific for our lives to be valuable, but the reality is all life is important.

Remember the second perspective – everything has value. All life is valuable because it presents you and others with opportunities to learn, improve and have more experiences. You provide value for people around you just by being yourself and living your life. They provide value for you by being themselves and living their lives.

Everything you do and every decision and action you take contributes to a ripple effect upon those around you.

Let's take reading this book as an example. Learning what you are learning in this book will already get you thinking differently, behaving differently and setting goals. Setting goals puts life in motion. It brings about new experiences where you learn, improve, have more experiences and contribute more to other people and how their lives unfold.

You do this by talking to others about your experiences, being observed by others as you have your experiences, or when they become a part of your new experience and create an impact on their life somehow.

You might inspire people to change too through what you're doing from learning in this book. You might reinforce their current beliefs or help them to start doubting their incorrect beliefs about life. You might even help them to upgrade and change their beliefs because of what you are doing. You are likely doing this with your children already if you have adopted some of the information taught by the Parental Stress Centre. Consequently your impact on them causes them to then make decisions, set goals and respond to their thoughts through action, goals and the continuing momentum of life.

Even if you hate this book you will still be contributing to other people's lives. You might tell a friend this book is rubbish and not to buy it. They may listen to you and not buy it and therefore not read what I have written. They won't do the exercises and will go off and have other experiences than what they would have had if they had bought the book and read it.

Whether they buy and read the book or not does not make their life more or less valuable, it just produces a result. If they read the book and did the things I suggest they will experience something. If they don't read the book they will just experience something else. Both of those pathways lead to both wanted and unwanted events because that's what life is about – ups and downs.

Understanding true self-worth is recognising that every moment of your life is valuable because you are learning through your experiences and because you are sharing what you've learnt and contributing who you are to the unfolding lives around you.

Your life is intrinsically valuable because you exist! There is nothing you need to be, do or have in order to be valuable. You are always making a difference to the lives of those around you. You are already important.

Consider this question for a moment – who takes the credit for bread being in your home?

When I ask this question to clients the most common answer I get is 'me. I buy the bread'.

But how did it get there? Who's responsible for the bread?

One might say the baker, the store owner or the cashier who sold the bread. Is it just those people or is it the wheat harvester too? Or is it the people who work in the silo, or the people who produce the wheat? Is it the milk producer or the cows that produce the milk that goes into the bread? Is it the person who makes the yeast or the janitor that keep these places clean so we eat it in a healthy way? Is it the delivery driver that delivers the bread? Is it the inventor of all the machinery that produces the bread, or all the people that played around with the ingredients that eventuated into the invention of bread? Or is it the parents who gave birth to all of these people who are associated with bread being in your home? Or is it their parents?

So who takes the credit for bread being in your home?

The answer – we all do. In one way or another we have all contributed to bread being available in stores because on a much larger scale we are all influencers of the bread making, delivery, purchasing or eating process that keeps bread making in motion.

Did you need to be, do or have any specific qualities to be an influencer of bread? No. All you did was be you with a preference for bread. That was enough to contribute to keeping the bread company going, the wheat being grown, cultivated, delivered, baked and sold.

The reality is your worth is intrinsic because you are part of the momentum of life unfolding – you are an integral part of the collective whole.

You often hear in spiritual circles how we are all individually responsible for the collective consciousness and the state of society. This is because who you are automatically creates a ripple effect in the lives of those who come into contact with you and that ripple effect continues out immeasurably beyond your conscious understanding.

Let's say you are on your own, taking some much needed time out. You are sitting in front of a large lake, trying to regain some serenity after the kids had been driving you crazy. One might argue that in this moment you aren't contributing to anyone.

However as you are contemplating your life you aimlessly throw a stone into the lake. The stone scares the platypus who shoots off in the water and scares the bird. The bird flies off into the path of an oncoming car two streets away. The driver of the car swerves and narrowly avoids driving off the edge of a cliff. He had just been driving away from his home after a rather nasty fight with his wife and he was angry – a usual state of being for him. This near accident with the cliff really shakes him. He realises he could have died. He begins to think about the way he had been acting. He realises he needs to change his life because he's so angry all of the time. He goes home and tells his wife he needs help and wants to save their marriage. They attend counselling, he improves and learns how to forgive his past and his family and even reunites with his father who he was estranged from for years. He cultivates a better relationship with his children. He completely changes his life and the relationships around him. As a result, when his children grow up and have children of their own the cycle of anger and dysfunction in their family stopped because they learnt a different way of being from their father.

This happened all because YOU threw one measly stone in the water when you were on your own!

Another example I like to share with people is of a movie called Sliding Doors with Gwyneth Paltrow. If you're not familiar with the movie it is about two potential lives that she could have had because of one seemingly insignificant event.

As the story goes Gwyneth's character gets fired from her job. After she packs up her things she rushes to get the train to go home to her partner. In one scenario a little boy drops a toy and she almost trips over him and as a result she misses her train. Because she missed her train she doesn't get home in time to catch her partner cheating on her. From here her life keeps going downhill, the relationship keeps getting worse, her partner keeps cheating on her behind her back and on it goes.

In the other scenario she doesn't trip over the little boy at the train station and catches her partner cheating on her. She leaves him, goes through a period of feeling down and out, but decides she will go into business for herself. She ends up having a really successful business, learns to believe in herself and meets another man who adores her.

Not only is it a classic movie that tells of lows leading to highs, unwanted situations providing value because it forced her to personally improve and an unwanted event leading to a wanted one, it also represents how significant the smallest moments of your life can be such an impact to someone else's life.

Although that little boy played a seemingly insignificant role in her life the impact he made was huge and led to a succession of events on her life story. You are doing that to others ALL of the time.

Even if you hadn't thrown the stone in the water in my first example and you were just away from your kids for a bit, that still creates experiences for your children and the person taking care of your children. They still learn, grow, experience and share their knowledge with others, participating in the momentum of life that you are at the centre of.

The reality is your life is always contributing to the lives of those around you whether you are conscious of it or not, because all of our experiences are linked.

Just by being you, you contribute to your child's life, your partner's life, your friends, other family, strangers, work colleagues, consumerism and acquaintances.

Everyone you come in contact with learns from their experiences of you. They learn how to do something or do it better (event learning). They may learn they need to improve themselves, or their experience of you may lead them to another high and a subsequent low, or a low with a subsequent high. They have ups and downs, learning and growing because of you. And that's happening whether you rate yourself as being a good or a bad influence.

You have no idea the magnitude of the role you play in the ripple effect of other people's journey. You are so important to life right now and you don't even realise it!

When you are succeeding, you are valuable to people. When you are making mistakes, you are valuable to people. When you are behaving in a way you don't like and wish you hadn't your life still has value.

You just don't feel like that because you have been indoctrinated to believe your worth is conditional upon getting life right. That's not self-worth, that's self-esteem – how you rate yourself in accordance with your beliefs.

When you truly understand self-worth and know there is nothing you need to be, do or have to be more worthy than you already are, then you tend to let go of your attachments. Life becomes what you want to experience, not what you feel like you have to experience in order to validate your worth.

So you are experiencing chaos in your current life? Well that just gives you an opportunity to learn how to manage life better.

So the kids are having a tantrum in the shopping centre? That doesn't mean anything about you as a person. Your child is learning she can't get her own way.

So you're not able to do the things you used to do? That just means you are experiencing something else in your life's play.

So you're bored, or not feeling fulfilled, or not having any fun? That doesn't mean your life is worth any less. This is just a stage you're going through and it's a call to do something different.

So what are you going to do about it?

Understanding true self-worth is recognising your life as it is right now is always valuable because of the inevitable impact you are always having on other people's lives.

You don't need to rate your life as good or bad because your rating is irrelevant. The experience you are having, whether enjoyable or not, is just an experience that is part of your highs and lows. It's teaching you something or providing the platform to give you other opportunities to learn and experience and it's contributing to the ripple effect of life unfolding for everyone around you. People need you to have certain life experiences and you need them to have yours.

Self-worth is the understanding that your life is ALWAYS valuable, not just when it meets the conditions of your life.

If you have a pulse, you have a purpose!

Your purpose is to be you with all your strengths and weaknesses, all your mistakes and successes and to be at the exact stage of personal development you are currently at right now! Because right now you are already making a difference! Who you are is ALWAYS enough.

Exercise Five
Evidence of your worth.

Make a list or contemplate as many different scenarios where you have contributed to the unfolding of life today. Consider the following:

- Who have you spoken to and what did you say?
- What tasks, chores or roles have you played in the family?
- How do you contribute to how the family functions?
- What are you teaching your children (highs and the lows that lead to more highs and lows)?
- Can you see how your undesirable behaviour has led to a lesson for you or your child in life?
- Can you see how your undesirable behaviour contributed to you doing something different that has led to your child benefiting from the experience?
- Have you used any products or technology today which may have contributed to a business?

- Have you posted something on Facebook or Twitter today?

- Did you encourage someone to do something?

- Have you convinced someone to change their mind or do something different which might have led them to experience something in their life?

- Have you been on the road today and contributed to other driver experiences?

- Have you spoken to your children, your friends, your husband?

- Have you NOT been somewhere you had said you'd be at a particular time?

- Have you heard someone say that because of you something else has happened (positive or not)?

- Have you had any wins today that taught you something you are likely to share with someone else?

- Have you had any losses or times where things didn't go the way you wanted them too that you are likely to share with someone else?

- Can you see evidence of how you have directly influenced someone's life by being who you are?

I could go on forever with these questions. Continue on with this line of thinking and keep finding evidence of how you are ALWAYS worthy just by being you.

Handling the difference between the reality of self-worth and the perceived reality of self-esteem.

Now we've gotten all warm and fuzzy about our worth and are feeling motivated to get out into the world and be our perfect selves, just as we are, I have to stop you for a minute to remind you of a very important point.

You just have one more thing to contend with – your judging mind.

Whether you feel good about yourself or not habitually comes from your beliefs about what makes you a good person or a bad person and the brain looks for evidence to match those beliefs.

As you now know, this is your self-esteem, how you rate yourself, and it fluctuates in accordance to how you are perceiving yourself in each moment.

This is a reality of the brain's function that you are not going to move past in a hurry.

As much as you'll want to adopt the 'I am 100 percent worthy' approach to life, you will need to provide yourself with loads of evidence and be very deliberate (conscious) about applying this new belief about yourself so the brain can learn to habitually believe this concept too.

There will be many times when your brain continues to judge as it always has and you are left feeling bad about yourself whenever you do something you wish you hadn't or when life throws you those unwanted events.

Rather than resisting this reality of the brain's judging function we just need to work *with* it.

This is where your awareness will come in to play. Be aware (conscious) of your fluctuating self-esteem and keep reminding yourself of the true essence of your worth by finding evidence of your constant contribution to the world as well as looking at the bigger picture of life's ups and downs and the learning and value that comes from all your experiences.

Finding evidence is going to be really important. For example, if you make a mistake that causes someone else pain (like flying off the handle at your children) your brain is pretty quickly going to habitually jump in to rate you as being a bad person (or parent).

This is where you need to be aware of your child-self's tendencies to rate you in low regard and re-educate her with the truth about self-worth alongside the other two new perspectives (life is a story of ups and downs; everything has value).

Your new story in your mind might go something like this:

"I didn't mean to hurt my child. I'm truly sorry for my actions. This is another reminder that I need to learn more

and practice more patience. I'm doing the best I can and I really am trying to learn to do this differently and make changes, but that's going to take time.

In the meantime, I will go and tell my child I am sorry and talk to them about my learning. That way they'll understand sometimes parents make mistakes too. They will learn it's okay to say sorry, we all make mistakes, and that learning something new takes practice. If I am honest about how I'm feeling and how I'm trying to change, then I will become an example of how to be more accepting of one's faults and mistakes and hopefully my child will more likely feel accepting of their own.

This situation, although unwanted (I really didn't want to yell at my child again), is still valuable to myself and my child. It is not a reflection of me being a bad person. Anger is just an issue I'm working through right now. Everyone has their issues they are working on."

We need to work *with* the reality of your current judgements on yourself and train the brain to judge unwanted events in a different way – that is, train the child-self to judge life with the three new perspectives.

When some people first hear this definition of self-worth they can become concerned that it gives people a licence to do whatever they want, whenever they want, without caring or considering anyone else's feelings– after all you'll just be contributing to highs and lows anyway, so it doesn't matter what you do, right? Why should you care about the effect you have on someone else's life when it will just lead to a high or low anyway?

However, remember the evaluation process we all go through. We experience our environment with the five senses. The data we receive gets evaluated by our brain with the current information we have stored. With an agenda of pursuing pleasure and avoiding pain and with the information accessed, the brain issues a response, which is how we feel and our re-ACTION to the event.

Whenever someone is ACTING (or re-acting) in a certain way, what do you think the evaluation process is behind that behaviour? It's an incorrect understanding of self-worth.

Hurtful actions really come from a fear of being unworthy. We've been taught to evaluate our worth as conditional. First you rate yourself as being worth less in some way and then you do something (reaction) to reinstate that worth through some action – you feel the need to assert your worth, be better than someone, shut them down to build you up, or you want to see their life as being worse than yours so you can feel better about your own. You want to prove your worth and achieve your goals, and you'll move anything (or anyone) that gets in your way.

But when you understand that there's nothing you need to specifically do in life to be worthy, life doesn't need to be asserted anymore. You feel so good about yourself and your life that you want to share this feeling with other people.

You begin to want everyone to feel as good as you do because this will be what connects you, makes you feel accepted, loved and continue the pursuit of feeling good. It wouldn't feel as good if you were the only one feeling this way so you actively try to help others to feel good too.

This is often why when you learn to accept and approve of yourself negative or dysfunctional relationships either change or separate because you just aren't connecting with them like you usually would. The dynamic has changed.

It might be the case that when you grasp this concept of self-worth you may set goals and make decisions that are different to your norm and others may experience the results of those decisions and be unhappy them. However, you won't go about it in a harmful or hurtful way because that just won't be your agenda anymore.

You'll be more likely to go out of your way to help them get what they want while you get what you want because you aren't trying to be better than them.

The need to break the moral code of being kind to one another simply won't be there. There will be no need to compete or be seen as better. There's no need to feel unlovable and want to punish other people for your hurts. You begin to accept your shortcomings as just opportunities to learn more or to be a contributor to the world of someone else.

You don't look for a life you should be having and feel resentful or jealous because of another's life because you are accepting your present life just as it is. You won't feel the need to assert your identity or defend it either.

There is no need for more money, more love, more acknowledgment, more things or more experiences because you are in full acceptance of what you have right now. Everything is acceptable just as it is.

That doesn't mean you won't ever want to change your reality though. However, any thoughts of lack are only met by a desire to seek out a new experience and then researching and planning how to do that. It becomes a want, not a need.

If you want more money, then you go about learning how to get it. You don't feel like your life is worth any less without it, you are just looking for ways to get that experience because you want it, not because you think you need it to validate your worth.

Emotions such as fear, resentment, judgement, anger, hostility, lack of forgiveness, guilt and every other painful emotion you can think of, all dissipate when you hold the understanding of true self-worth, the understanding that there's value in everything and the understanding of life's continuation of ups and downs.

You also begin to understand that other people's behaviour is just a result of their beliefs and their self-worth attachments, so you won't personalise their behaviour either and want to retaliate against it. You won't want to harm them or feel ill towards them because you will see the hurt behind their behaviours and identify with their pain, for you have felt that way yourself.

You learn to equalise yourself with the other person who's done wrong by you and see yourself in them, because at some point you have acted out of those same insecurities and incorrect beliefs. You begin to feel compassionate towards them, not hurtful. You begin to say, "That person is in pain. That's why they behave that way. It's actually not about me. It's actually about them and how they feel about themselves."

Another interesting thing happens too when you recognise your inherent worth. You get more real and people want to love you, be affectionate towards you and be kind to you. You aren't trying to assert yourself or make yourself better by making them feel worse and because you accept all your strengths, weaknesses, mistakes and personality traits just as they are you're not judging their faults anymore.

Everyone wants to feel accepted too, so you end up becoming a safe person to be around. Other people feel free to be who they are without judgement. All of a sudden your relationships become a lot closer and have a lot more depth to them.

You start to become part of a loop of more love and acceptance than you've ever had before, and you're not even trying to get it.

Working with the reality of your judging mind and the reality of your current rating system (your self-esteem) without resistance will be the key to transition into this self-accepting, always-worthy state of being.

In order to physically retrain the brain to view life in alignment with the three perspectives (life is a story of ups and downs, everything has value and you are always 100 percent worthy), you will need to consistently and repetitively take the following steps:

- Become aware of how you are feeling.

- Consciously recognise the old habit of rating yourself and attaching your worth to any identity or 'right' life thinking.

- Recognise this thinking as your child-self (and who you've name it as).

- Acknowledge that this old thinking does not represent reality.

- Think about the current situation within the three new perspectives.

- Find evidence of why these three new perspectives are reality.

Exercise Six
Create a new story.

Pick a moment from your day where you have been caught up in thinking you have lost your identity or when you don't think your life is going right.

Follow the 6 steps above and create a new story (perspective) of how you could view this situation through the new three perspectives.

Note: These concepts are dealt with on a much deeper scale in our BE the Change webinar series. I discuss in more detail the set-up of habitual thinking, identifying the specific beliefs behind your stress and how to change it. You will also get an even deeper understanding of stress, depression and anxiety and how to change to live a happier life.

Chapter Five

Step Three: Aim – what do I want?

When you first purchased this book you wanted to know how to regain your lost identity. Like anything with the *Parental Stress Centre*, you will leave with a much deeper perspective than you came for.

This is because it is vital to understand yourself in order to live a more peaceful and fulfilling life.

You now have the understanding of how you attach your worth to your identity and how it is no longer necessary to keep doing that in order to be worthy. You now know (at least logically) that you are always 100 percent worthy.

However, as we discussed in the last chapter the judging mind is always going to want to pursue ways to feel good (pleasure) and avoid feeling bad (emotional pain), and this is unlikely to change. If you do try to change this it's going to take a lot of time and commitment as you are trying to undo a generational trait that goes back to the beginning of mankind!

We will probably always want our self-image to be a certain way to a degree although how we want to be perceived will change as we grow older.

We will probably always want to feel self-confident in what we do and want to feel good about getting things right.

We will always want people to treat us well and be upset to some degree if they aren't. We want to feel good about ourselves and have the ability to teach people how to treat us kindly.

But now we understand the difference between our self-esteem and our inherent, unchanging self-worth there's a big difference.

We are now talking about what we want to experience, not what we feel we have to experience in order to feel worthy. When you understand that your life is intrinsically worthy at all times and there's nothing you need to do, be or have, you can now invest your attention towards what you want to experience in your life.

You're not spending all your energy focussed on what's not happening. When you use the three new perspectives you are in alignment with reality and you are accepting of it.

It doesn't mean you'll always like your reality, but you will be able to accept that it is just a scene in your life's play, it is teaching you something and it doesn't mean anything about your worth.

Now you can move on to making changes to it.

If you are unhappy about your self-image, don't feel confident in a particular area of life or have a low level of self-respect or difficulties in relationship, now that you are aligned with the reality of where you are at, you can decide what you want in these areas.

A healthy view of your self-image.

How do I want to be perceived by the world? What do I want to look like? What sort of person do I want to be seen as? What sort of legacy do I want to leave in this lifetime? These become the new questions you ask yourself without the attachment to what other people think of you.

The reality is sometimes you will be perceived in that way and sometimes you won't (highs and lows) because people are perceiving you with their beliefs, not yours.

Because you understand your self-worth is not attached to anyone's beliefs about the right image, your self-image goals become about how you *want* to be in the world, not what you should look like to the world.

A healthy level of self-confidence.

Continue working on being confident in the areas of life you don't feel confident in but with the knowledge that some things you'll be good at, some things you won't be good at and others will just be about learning and practicing new ways.

If you *want* to experience being better at something than you are, do it because you want to be better at it not because you have to prove your worth.

A true understanding of self-worth means you feel okay about not knowing something and you feel confident to say so. There's no need to pretend you know something when you don't.

Your self-worth is never attached to what you know or how you do things. You are always worthy because you exist and because of the ripple effect. Life is just a series of things you experience and learn from.

A healthy level of self-respect.

We want people to treat us kindly. The dynamic between you and another person has come about because both of you contributed to it. If the dynamic between you is unhealthy your participation in the current dynamic has likely come about because at some level you have believed you are less than worthy and haven't learnt the skills of teaching people how you would like to be treated.

It's likely you aren't even treating yourself the way you would like to be treated.

As well as that, the other person has contributed to the dynamic too by responding to you in accordance with their beliefs and how they want to be treated. Their behaviour has nothing to do with you being worthy or not. It actually speaks volumes about how they feel about themselves to be treating you that way. Why do we put someone down? In order to feel better about ourselves.

However, because of your contribution, you have also played a part in the creation of that dynamic. If it was all their fault and you did understand your true worth you would have walked away long ago.

Understanding your part in your current relationship with someone can turn your attention towards what you might need to learn and implement in your life to create more harmonious relationships and learn how to teach people how to treat you better.

Everything has value and sometimes events like being treated poorly wakes you up and lets you know that you need to learn something new in this area to improve and change yourself personally. It reminds you that your new learning will lead to new experiences – like having quality relationships for example. Remember my favourite saying, how do we know what to do until we've experienced what NOT to do?

If you are having issues with your marital relationships see our website under Successful Relationships for further help.

With your fundamental knowledge of the reality of self-worth and the reality of your self-esteem (how you rate yourself) you can now embrace these two understandings and begin to deliberately create the life you want to live and the identity that you wish to experience.

Except now you are doing it with no attachments.

This is where you are ready to continue on with the rest of the Mind TRACK to happiness process and redefine your 'lost' identity.

What do I want?

We all have some kind of vision of who we want to be and what we want to get out of life and I don't mean materialistically.

Newton Faulker in his song "Dream catch me" said:

There's a place I go
When I'm alone
Do anything I want, be anyone I want to be

There is a place within all of us where we dream of life being a particular way. We know the sort of person we want to be, the legacy we want to leave (or at least know we want to leave one), and we know what we'd like to experience in our lives that will create more peace within ourselves. But often we are too scared to go there.

The fear comes from believing you might be judged as not good enough or you may be rejected for being who you want to be. Perhaps you fear life will go wrong or you will miss out on some other experience? Perhaps you fear you won't know how to deal with life if you get what you want? Perhaps you fear success just as much as your fear failure?

When you get real quiet and you contemplate the difference between the life you want and the life you have, deep down you already know what your fear is and ultimately it will have its roots in some incorrect belief about the potential for you or your life to be worth less.

The mind prefers to stick with what it knows. Even if it is a painful reality you are experiencing there is safety because you know you can deal with this bad experience, and the fear of the unknown keeps you stuck there.

But when the pain of your current reality outweighs the fear of an unknown future changes will be made.

Now is the time to make that change. Now, perhaps even for the first time in your life, it is time to let go of the old, indoctrinated fearful thinking and begin to create and embrace a new life that aligns with part of you that is screaming to be set free.

Parenthood opens us up to a completely new world and forces you to embark on unknown territory. That's why you feel you have lost your identity. You are no longer able to identify what used to define who you are and that scares you. You don't have a reference point for this new reality and you fear you may not get it right. You have lost what you thought made you good enough, worthy enough or important enough to the world and you don't know what to do with yourself. Or perhaps you never felt good enough and you fear you won't be good enough for your children either.

When we feel this fear we believe the answer is to control our image so we are perceived by others in a way that will make us look worthy, but it conflicts with what we want to be.

You want to be a career mum, but you think you should be a stay at home mum. You want to be a stay at home mum, but you think you should be contributing to the household income or you have been taught you have to pull your weight.

You want to raise your children with completely different morals and values to your cultural heritage or in a different way to society, but you fear you will be ostracised from your family or judged by others.

You feel it's time to move on from a relationship, but you fear the unknown of what will happen if you do, or what people will say. Or you believe it will mess up your child's life.

You want to change as a person but you fear you will no longer be able to connect with your partner, or with the friends you have. You may have even tried to change, but realised you won't have anything in common with those you are currently close to, so you reverted back to your old self.

You just know there is a different place you want to be personally, spiritually or emotionally yet you still repeat the same patterns and make the same decisions that cause the same pain. Your fear of change has paralysed you from doing anything.

The things you are experiencing as a parent probably aren't even exclusive to parenting. Chances are you have been hiding away from what you want for a long time. It's just now you've become a parent, your circumstances have now made it too unbearable to keep up the façade.

Becoming a parent is notorious for bringing out deep seated issues that have previously laid dormant. This is because we often no longer have the distraction of work, social outings and free time that we would usually fill up with noise to distract us.

If we were unhappy with ourselves before, it hits us in the face with full force now that we are thinking about how we are going to raise our children with the values and peace we don't even feel ourselves.

That part of you that has been trapped by conditional thinking and a façade of happiness starts to scream at you. *"Something needs to change! Come on, let's do this. Not just for yourself, but for your children. I can't keep living like this. I can't keep living this lie!"*

It becomes harder and harder to fake being happy, fulfilled or at peace because you aren't being real with the person you truly are. You are too fixated on the person you think you should be. You're fixated on your rating system and giving your worth away to chance, hoping someone else's belief system will deem you as good enough.

But all that can change right now. Stop... take a breath.

Relax.

Let's reconnect with our three new perspectives;

- Life is a story of ups and downs.
- There's value in everything.
- You are always 100 percent worthy.

Remind yourself of these concepts. Now there is nothing left to fear. You are totally free to be who you want to be. You are no longer restricted by someone else's beliefs of who you should be or how you should perform or behave.

You are free to be you.

This won't mean you will go about doing what you want to do without any concern for anyone else, because that would be selfish. Selfishness will only alienate you further from the world and take you further from the love, peace and connection you are searching for.

Realise right now you can have what you want AND still create close and fulfilling relationships. In fact you are more likely to create those relationships when you get real with yourself and don't put up those pretences and facades.

There is likely to be people who won't like you changing, but that's okay. That's their journey. You will find the more true you are to yourself, others around you will either change too, or move away from you in one way or another and be replaced with new, much more fulfilling relationships.

This aim step is about deciding who *you* want to be in this life.

I was going to create an exercise consisting of a list of questions to help you to decide who you want to be, however I was randomly reminded of the song "Dream Catch Me" and I have decided you already know who you want to be, what morals, values and standards you want to live by. You already know who you are when you are alone and take off those masks to the world, you just need to say it out loud, write it down and get real with yourself.

You just need to take some time to get quiet, get reflective and decide.

Now you know that your life is always valuable, who do you *want* to be? What do you *want* from life? How do you *want* to live it in order to experience the joy and peace you are looking for? How do you *want* to be an example for your children so they feel free to be themselves too?

This aim step is to establish: What do *I want*?

Exercise Seven
Write your eulogy.

Write a eulogy of the life you would like to have from here on in. Contemplate what you would like someone to say about you and the life you have lead after you've grown old and passed on.

Describe in great detail what your character was like, who you were to other people, what you believed in and stood for, what sort of parent you were and what sort of experiences you had.

How would you like to be remembered for living life?

Stay aware of the tendency to fall into character traits that have been indoctrinated within you as someone you 'should' be. As an adult those indoctrinations don't apply anymore. YOU get to decide what you want.

Write this eulogy for yourself and then take some time to read back on it and consciously make the decisions to create this life for yourself.

Chapter Six

Step Four: Choices – How do I get what I want?

I read a quote at the beginning of 2013 that completely changed the way I viewed the things that I wanted. It said:

"The difference between rich people and poor people is, poor people want to be rich, rich people are committed to being rich."

Highlighting the difference between wanting and committing really struck a chord with me. I realised this quote could apply to so many things.

So often we want things, but we never commit to them. We never put in the effort. We don't set what we want as a goal, it just stays as a wish. We don't research how to get what we want. We don't take action and, as a result, we don't get what we want.

The Choices step of the process is all about figuring out HOW to get what we've stated in the Aim step and to make a conscious commitment to seek out those answers and pursue your goal until you get it.

How do you go about becoming the person you want to be?

I would love to be able to give you the step-by-step guide to answering this question, but, as you may have already gathered, there is no clear cut answer.

Your purpose in life is to be you, exactly as you are right now. Whatever you do and however you grow as a human being that too will also be purposeful.

Whenever you want something but you don't know how to get it, the best way is to learn off someone who has done it. Who has been through what you have been through and would be able to give you the knowledge, guidance and tools to get you where you want to go?

When you put your attention on what you want, you begin to find evidence of the information you need to get it. Remember my car analogy? When you thought about buying a new car you started to notice that make and model everywhere.

The same will apply when you focus your attention on getting what you want.

If you want to change the person you are or change your life to have new experiences, then start searching for the information that will teach you how.

If you are struggling in the area of relationships then find resources that will teach you how to communicate better, be assertive, negotiate and compromise.

If you are struggling in the area of self-confidence then take courses and read books on how to feel differently about yourself. Do the exercises they suggest to start practicing being that different person.

If self-image is your struggle and there is a gap between the way you want to look and the way you do look then get serious about learning what you need to change. If weight is your issue, rather than trying another fad diet, look for information about how to retrain your brain to think about food differently and create a healthy relationship with food.

If you want to pursue a career, either outside of the home or while raising your children, start doing some research. There is always someone doing what you want to do. Seek them out, ask questions and learn from them. It might take some time, but that's all part of the journey.

Start looking for the information and the brain will start to find it in the most random places.

The real purpose of goals.

As you go about searching for information to help you change your life, find your identity and reach your goals, it's important to understand the real purpose of goals.

Often we start rating our life as being worth less because things aren't happening as quickly as we want them to. We get impatient and feel like giving up. We are essentially saying, "I feel like I'm never going to make my life better." However what sort of thinking is this? Is it self-esteem or is it self-worth?

What makes life valuable is NOT the achievement of goals. In fact, that's not even the purpose of setting a goal.

The purpose of a goal is NOT about the achievement of them at all. That's right you achievers out there. This upgrade is going to do your head in if you've continually attached your worth to reaching your goals.

Although the intention of a goal is to achieve it's not the essential outcome of the goal that creates value.

Goals set life in motion. By setting a goal you go about having a whole new set of experiences. You learn, try new things, fail and succeed, and all the while you are learning and growing and contributing new experiences to those around you.

You set goals every day. You get out of bed. You brush your teeth. You get in your car and drive somewhere. You make plans for the weekend. In fact, when you look at all the goals you set on a daily basis, you actually achieve 90 percent of the goals you set in life.

You're not such a failure after all.

Goals don't have to be big in order for them to have value. Setting a goal and even uttering one word about it or taking one step towards that goal is already creating the ripple effect that makes your life valuable.

Getting to the goal, not getting the goal, being on the way to the goal or even life after not reaching a goal, these experiences ALL make up your life's story and all of it has value because of what you learn, how you improve and where it leads you next.

So when it comes to this choices step, don't get caught up in the right pathway to take to get to your goal because everything you do will be useful. As you continue gathering information about the 'how to' part of getting to your goal just keep yourself in the current moment and in the natural flow of life.

Just keep learning, researching, asking and recognising that your shortcomings are just opportunities to get more information on how to 'do' life.

Exercise Eight
Make time for research.

Set aside some time to start establishing what you need to learn and research in order to get what you want to experience in your life.

If it's money, how do you earn more money?

If it's confidence, how do you learn to increase confidence?

If it's a new career, what do you need to do in order to take that career?

Even if you don't know what you want, setting an intention to start searching for what might interest you will get the brain searching for information to give you the answer.

Stay aware of conversations you hear, books, seminars or videos that teach you how to do what you want to do. Take notice of little messages from movies that seem to resonate with you or cause a stir. Find other people who are doing what you want to do and ask them how they did it so you can copy it.

Collate all the information you can about your goals to get ready for the final step of the TRACK process – Know your Plan and action it.

Chapter Seven

Step Five – Know your plan and action it.

Nothing changes if nothing changes. How many times have you contemplated the idea of doing something in your life, you may even have the information or paperwork sitting right next to you, but the fear of taking that leap stops you from doing it.

It is my hope that through this book you will have released some of those fears and are beginning to embrace the idea of just taking the plunge and doing what you are considering doing to change your life and live it in more alignment to a peaceful existence.

Take the information you have gathered in step four and TAKE ACTION. Don't look back. Don't fear the future. Live for right now.

Formulate the steps that need to be taken to meet your goal into an action plan and start taking those steps today! If you want help with how to do that, then my two books, *A parent's guide to knowing what you want and how to get it* and *A parent's guide to balance and getting more YOU time* will be perfect compliments to this book.

No more contemplating. No more procrastinating. There's nothing to fear, nothing to lose (in terms of your value) and everything to gain.

Most people know what they need to do in order to make changes but they just don't do it. Are you going to just want what you want or are you going to commit to it?

Exercise Nine
What is your plan?

From the information found in Step four, formulate a plan of the steps you need to take to begin working towards your goal.

Be clear and specific. Create mini goals or milestones to help you to gauge your progress.

One final note on creating your plan. Be flexible. The reality is life doesn't always go to plan and sometimes we need to re-plan, seek out new ways when things don't work.

There is no one pathway leading to your 'right path' because there is no right way for life to unfold. Be flexible about how you get to your goal and don't be afraid to revise your plan or even change your goal altogether.

Life is just a series of experiences that make up your life. Sometimes we get new information that makes us reassess what we want and leads us in a totally new direction.

You may start to create an action plan to leave your partner, but when it gets to the telling your partner bit, he/she might realise things are serious and want to work on your marriage. Be flexible and maybe give this a go instead.

On the flip side you may start to research ways to improve your relationship and find you no longer have anything in common with your partner and wish to part ways. Life could take you in that direction too.

You might feel like you want to be a stay-at-home parent, make all the plans, rearrange your finances and become a stay at home parent, only to discover you don't like it.

You might start a business or studies and then get information on a new venture that would inspire you more and decide to take that option.

You might decide to be a fitness fanatic and finally get the body you've always wanted, but once you get there, realise you don't necessarily like the attention you get or you don't like how much time it takes to keep up that level of fitness and you may decide to pull it back a notch.

Bottom line – don't get attached to your plan or your goal. You can't get life wrong. Your goals just set life in motion and create experiences that push you to learn, grow and contribute to life.

When you are ninety-something years old and looking back on your life you are just going to see a series of events that played out in your unique life story. Some events you wanted and were planned. Some events were not wanted and unplanned. Some events you did plan but ended up being unwanted. Some events you didn't plan but ended up being wanted.

It's just a story and no one event EVER defines your life's worth.

Chapter Eight

Just be YOU.

'I don't know who I am anymore'.

The brain loves to identify with what's always happened. It is a creature of habit. No different to a computer, it will respond to life in the way it has been programmed to.

Feeling lost is just your brain's way of saying it has lost its ability to pursue pleasure or avoid pain in the way it's become accustomed to using past conditioning and physical neural pathways.

This can be a great thing – an opportunity to wake up and start to redesign your life.

As a parent you have moved into a new phase of your life. It is one that forces you to ask the deeper questions about life and your place in the world and it is one where you are forced to leave behind most of what you know, or at least how you used to play out what you know.

It is an opportunity to come into yourself, mature and grow spiritually and emotionally.

On some level the ground feels shaky after having children so we will step up to the plate and develop ourselves personally so we can help our children do the same.

Our brain wants to live in the past. It wants to hold onto beliefs about how things should have been different.

It wants to judge your worth as conditional according to what you've learnt.

There are so many of us living with attachments to how we think we must live our lives, being determined not to be worth less like we rate our parents to be, and we get attached to that way of being.

Don't stay trapped in your past with those incorrect beliefs taught to you by someone who didn't know any better. You just don't need to live with these lies.

Society is riddled with dysfunction because we're all participating in the same cycle of feeling worth less and trying desperately to regain something that hasn't even been lost.

We are drowning in our own conditional thinking and we're projecting it onto those around us, either knowingly or unknowingly.

You create a ripple effect right now being the person that you are – faults and all. While we need to recognise our faults, accept where we are in our development and continue learning to improve ourselves, we must also keep focussed on the bigger goal.

If you could change anything in the world, anything at all, many would want to change the world to be a more peaceful place.

Well that peace starts with you. When you *commit* to a more peaceful life and you dedicate yourself to finding out how you can feel more at peace you will already be contributing to that peaceful world you wish to live in.

This is where Ghandi says: *"Be the Change you wish to see in your world".*

Who takes the credit for the bread? We all do.

Set your goals, accept your life as it is without casting degrading judgments, ridicule or criticism, but don't remain stuck there. Learn, grow and keep your eye on the much larger picture – a more peaceful life.

Your children need you to be more at peace with yourself because that's how they will learn to be more at peace with themselves.

If you think your personal development and learning to be accepting of your personal identity is a selfish venture, think again.

Who you are is so important to the world!

When you step away from the indoctrinations of your past and you begin to deliberately live life in alignment with our three new perspectives – life is a journey of ups and downs, everything has value, you are always 100 percent worthy – life does become more enjoyable. You do become more accepting of yourself and others. You do become kinder, more compassionate, empathetic, giving and loving and you ripple that out into the world immeasurably.

You came to this book looking to discover who you are now that you are a parent. Well who you are is a contributor in society who is always valuable no matter what you do.

You're not valuable because of what you know, what you do or how you do it. You are valuable because you are here doing it!

If you stay as you are right now that won't mean your ripple effect will be right or wrong. It will just cause an effect.

Stay stuck in your fear, self-criticisms, judgements of others, hatefulness, unkindness, sadness, loneliness, depression and anxiety and you will contribute to that mind set staying in the world. You will speak, do and behave in alignment with beliefs that produce more fear, self-criticism, judgement, hatefulness, unkindness, sadness, loneliness, depression and anxiety thinking, doing and behaving in society.

It's not wrong. Other people will still learn and grow from it. You will still learn and grow from it. We will all have experiences from it. Life will go on and your life will still be hugely valuable.

However, if you discover yourself to be a peaceful person able to accept yourself and others around you, are able to be kind, compassionate, empathetic, giving, humorous, fun loving, adventurous and an inspiring person who loves life, you will create a ripple effect that is immeasurable too.

You will contribute to the shift taking place in the world where other people are realising it is safe to let go of this fear, embrace their true self-worth and be kind, compassionate, empathetic, fun loving and love life too. This is not the right way either. People will still learn from this way of living. You will still learn from it. We will all have experiences from it. Life will go on and your life will still be hugely valuable.

The question is – which life do you *want* to live? Which legacy do you *want* to leave for your friends, your family, your children and everyone you come in contact with?

When the curtains close on your life's play, no matter what you have or haven't done, your life will leave a legacy that will ripple out immeasurably to millions of lives for many years to come.

The question isn't who am I? The question is, who do I *want* to be?

What's stopping you from achieving your vision? What do you need to learn? And what are you going to DO to initiate a plan to change?

You are an adult now not a child anymore. You get to call the shots and within this book you have learnt how to understand why you do what you do, where it comes from and how you can start changing it.

Don't let it stop here when you close this book. Keep saturating your conscious brain with information, learning and personal development. Read more books, attend courses, join groups, hang around people who think like this and keep taking action towards understanding and changing those conditional beliefs that keep you stuck in fear and painful emotions. Keep working towards being the identity you want to experience in this life.

Because who you are makes a difference.
So what sort of difference do you want to make?

"When you are inspired...
dormant forces, faculties and talents become alive,
and you discover yourself to be a greater person
by far than you ever dreamed yourself to be."

PATANJALI

PARENTAL STRESS CENTRE

www.parentalstress.com.au

More Resources available from
The Parental Stress Centre

Books

- The Happy Mum Handbook

- The 28 Day Tame you Temper Parenting Challenge

- A Parent's Guide to Finding your lost identity
  (and discovering your personal peace)

- A Parent's Guide to Balance and getting more YOU time

Video Programs

- BE the Change Video Series
  Find your peace and calm, then teach it to your children

- Stress Free Parenting Program
  The rational and realistic approach to parenting that no one's ever shown you

- What's In it for Me Video Program
  The Relationship Repair series

- The 12 week Postnatal Depression Recovery Program

- The Tame your Temper Video Program

- The Time for Everything Video Program

www.ingramcontent.com/pod-product-compliance
Lightning Source LLC
Chambersburg PA
CBHW070816100426
42742CB00012B/2377